Sarah Caplin read Social Sciences at the University of York. She decided to become a solicitor and was admitted in January 1981. But by that time she was already working as a Research Assistant Trainee at the BBC. As an R.A.T. she worked on programmes ranging from late night chat shows to serious current affairs. She has directed films and produced studio programmes for the past four years. Now she is based permanently in the Documentary Features department and was an associate producer of *Drugwatch*.

Shaun Woodward lives and works in London. After leaving Cambridge University where he read English and took a Double First, he worked as a parliamentary lobbyist for the National Consumer Council. He first worked in television as a researcher for *That's Life*. He has worked as a reporter for *Newsnight* and the BBC series *That's Family Life* before becoming associate producer for *Newsnight*. He has published two books previously: *That's Life Survey on Tranquillisers* and *Ben: The Story of Ben Hardwick*, which was number one in the bestseller lists in 1985. He has just finished preparing a *That's Life* guide on *How to Complain* and is currently working on his first novel.

Drugwatch: Just Say No

Sarah Caplin and Shaun Woodward

By arrangement with the British
Broadcasting Corporation

CORGI BOOKS

DRUGWATCH: JUST SAY NO
A CORGI BOOK 0 552 12820 1

First publication in Great Britain

PRINTING HISTORY
Corgi edition published 1986

Foreword Copyright © Esther Rantzen

Text Copyright © Sarah Caplin and Shaun Woodward 1986

This book is set in 10/11pt Sabon

Corgi Books are published by Transworld Publishers Ltd.,
61-63 Uxbridge Road, Ealing, London W5 5SA,
in Australia by Transworld Publishers (Aust.) Pty. Ltd.,
26 Harley Crescent, Condell Park, NSW 2200, and in New
Zealand by Transworld Publishers (N.Z.) Ltd., Cnr. Moselle
and Waipareira Avenues, Henderson, Auckland.

Made and printed in Great Britain by
Hunt Barnard Printing Ltd., Aylesbury, Bucks.

To Adam

CONTENTS

7

FOREWORD

When *That's Life*, the BBC TV consumer programme, embarked on a survey into drug-taking in Britain, no one really knew what pattern would emerge. Of course individual tragic cases, usually heroin addicts, had already hit the headlines. There had also been a good deal of research usually based on the patients in drug treatment units. However, because television reaches straight into living-rooms all over the country, drug-takers who had never been part of the official statistics before, because they were not known to the police or the medical profession, took part in the *That's Life* survey. More than two thousand drug takers and their families provided frank, vivid information, describing their lives and their drug-taking. Those replies became the basis of the *Drugwatch* programme on BBC 1 in July 1985, and the follow-up programmes that developed from it. We who worked on those programmes owe the individuals and their families who wrote to us with such honesty, revealing many painful facts, a great debt of gratitude.

The picture revealed by the survey was both tragic and hopeful. Tragic because so many young lives are destroyed by addiction. Hopeful, because addiction is not necessarily the end of the line. One teenage girl wrote, 'As the months went by I was slowly killing myself. It was burglary by day, on the game at night, to pay for heroin – I was spending over £100 a day. I thought there was no way I could kick the habit – you know what they say, "once an addict, always an addict".' She was fifteen when she wrote those words, and yet she did kick the habit, she has now been drug-free for a year. It has taken a great effort of will, but her life now, although not perfect, (after all, whose life ever is), has become the crime-free life of a normal teenager. She is not unique. Half the users in the survey have also managed to break free from their drugs. Many addicts cured themselves, on their own, without treatment. So although addiction frequently leads to crime, can lead to death, often breaks up families and shatters lives, once an addict is *not* always an addict.

There are other lessons in this book for everyone. The fact, for instance, that drug-taking often begins so early, among young schoolchildren. The fact also that their drugs come first from friends, not dealers. Those first drugs are taken very often in a young person's own home, or the home of a friend. The drugs that seem to be the most dangerous include not just heroin or cocaine, but a wide range, particularly the amphetamines – 'speed'. Indeed, according to the survey, even cannabis has created addicts and wrecked lives.

The parents and families who took part in the survey felt a desperate need for support and advice. The drug users themselves tell us, with savage regret, how ignorant they were about the effects and dangers of the drugs they took, when they were first offered. Filling that information gap with clear, unhysterical facts became the aim of this excellent book. The authors – composers of the survey and associate producers of the *Drugwatch* programme – believe that forewarned is forearmed. The information in this book will help families all over the country, will encourage young people so that they can 'Just Say No' to drugs – this vital information may indeed save lives.

Esther Rantzen
December 1985

ACKNOWLEDGEMENTS

The authors would like to thank all the drug users, their families and friends who took part in the *Drugwatch* survey, without whose considerable courage and effort this book would not have been possible. We would particularly like to thank Melanie and Kay Rodie for their very special contributions.

Dr John Strang, David Turner and Dr Richard Hartnoll provided us with their expertise and were extremely patient as we plied them with endless questions. Our grateful thanks to them.

We cannot forget that the original idea for the programme was Michael Grade's – the Controller of BBC 1. Without his support neither the programme nor this book would have been produced.

Finally, our thanks to the *Drugwatch* team: Ritchic Cogan, Anne Webber, Joanna Clinton Davis, Simon Gallimore, Ann Laking, Kate Macky and Tricia Ambrose, without whom *Drugwatch* would never have got on the air and to Esther Rantzen and Nick Ross who made it such a success.

INTRODUCTION

At least four million people in Britain have tried drugs – from cannabis to speed, from heroin to cocaine.

Most of these people started taking drugs whilst they were still at school, living at home with their parents; they are young, impressionable and for some of them drugs have had a devastating effect on their lives.

Drug-taking in this country is a serious problem, a problem which for those who become hooked can destroy not only their own lives but the lives of those with whom they live. Drug-taking becomes a crisis which the entire family must face.

Few of us understand drugs. The word 'drugs' itself conjures up exotic images – altered states of consciousness, hallucinations, unnatural feelings of contentment and well-being as well as terrifying 'bad trips'. Yet drugs are pleasurable, so pleasurable that users will risk a great deal to ensure an uninterrupted supply. Drugs are dangerous because they are pleasurable – and this is a fact that is often overlooked. We know very little about why people take them, what happens to them when they do and why only some become hooked. And when drug users encounter problems we know very little about how to get advice or help and particularly where to get treatment.

What can we do? Undoubtedly the most important step we can take is to try and find answers to some of these questions. Ignorance is as much at the root of the present crisis as the dealings of the drug barons who push narcotics into countries throughout the world.

Some people think our only hope is to administer tougher sentences to pushers and to ensure greater customs and police control. But is this the answer? What can we do to try and stop young people abusing drugs and, more crucially, prevent them from experimenting in the first place?

To look at these questions, to try and understand the reality of the drug problem in Britain today, the BBC commissioned *Drugwatch*. Based on a survey of over two thousand drug users and their families, the programme looked at the reasons why people try drugs. It asked what kind of people are likely to try them, what happens when they experiment and when some become hooked, what help exists for those who want to stop taking drugs and whether anything can be done to prevent people starting to take them in the first place.

The survey was the most extensive study of drug use ever to be carried out in Britain, and the information in *Drugwatch* was based upon the survey, information from those with direct experience of taking drugs. To back up and develop this information we consulted researchers and drug experts throughout Britain and in the United States.

This book is based upon the *Drugwatch* programme. Drug-taking is a very frightening problem. It is a problem, a bit like crime, that will never be 'solved', but there are ways in which the problem might be alleviated and this book will look at those ways.

In the first part of the book we tell the story of Melanie, the girl who thought she would never take drugs, but then became so hooked she believed she would never live to be twenty-one. In the next part we look in detail at the stories and information that emerged from the *Drugwatch* survey – what drugs people take, why they start, how they become hooked and then how life changes, how to get help and, most importantly, how to prevent people ever starting. In the final section we have put together information about how and where to get help and have reproduced the survey.

How the Survey Came About
In February *That's Life* told the story of a young girl who had become hooked on heroin. To pay for her very expensive

habit she became a prostitute, stole from her friends and family and almost died. Her story struck a chord in homes and families throughout the country. The programme asked viewers who had experience of drugs to write in and help compile a picture of drug abuse in Britain.

Over three thousand people wrote agreeing to take part. With the advice of the Drug Indicators Project, a survey was designed. It was in two parts. One for the drug user; one for the family or close friend of the drug user. We hoped by sending both parts to the person who had applied for a questionnaire we might be able to put together a complete picture of the drug user's life from his own and his family's point of view.

Everyone who took part was guaranteed absolute confidentiality. It was a long and detailed survey, with over fifty questions to answer. Some people thought we were asking for too much information and that we would have few completed surveys. They were wrong. We received nearly two thousand surveys which had been completed with great care and attention to detail by users and their families. A number of them told us that they had never before talked (or written) about the problems drugs had created for them and were grateful for the opportunity of setting out their experiences and offering advice based on them.

The information was read and analysed and the statistics were fed through a computer. The result was a comprehensive picture of drug-taking in Britain in the mid 1980s.

Here is just a taste:

- most people start experimenting while still at school and living at home with their parents

- half the users in our survey have tried heroin

- four out of five people in our survey have tried speed – a drug which like heroin can create addicts and, in turn, very serious problems for the user

- most people in our survey had used lots of different drugs; the *average* number of drugs they had tried was ten

- heroin led to crime in nearly every case

But there was a strong message of hope:

- half the drug users in the survey told us they had given up drugs, many had managed on their own without treatment

And when asked what could be done to help control the drug problem, drug users and their families had clear, strong advice

- more education in school
- more publicity about the dangers of drugs

What drugs are we talking about?
In the survey we asked people to tell us about drugs they had tried which were not prescribed by a doctor. We were interested in illegal drug taking. However there is no doubt that there are a whole range of substances which can be used quite legally which are just as damaging – tranquillisers, solvents, glue and many others. A picture of the devastation which these can bring about also emerged from the survey.

The most common drug is cannabis. Cannabis comes in many forms and is known by many names. Sometimes you hear about marijuana or grass – the dried leaves. Hash or hashish is the resin of Thai sticks. To smoke it, it is powdered and usually mixed up with tobacco. Cannabis is cheap. A 'joint' of cannabis will cost about £1·50. You can tell if someone is smoking it because it smells quite different to cigarettes: it has a sweet smell, not at all pungent. Like cigarettes, smoking cannabis can lead to cancer. Like alcohol it causes injury and death because whilst under the influence of cannabis you are much more likely to meet with accidents.

In the sixties we heard a lot about LSD or acid. It comes in many forms and is not difficult to obtain. Sometimes it appears as little microdots, which are multi-coloured 'tabs' and are most easily taken on a sugar lump. It's cheap; a 'trip' on LSD will cost about £2·00. Many people try it. The results can be very different. LSD produces hallucinations; some good, some bad, but it can make you do crazy and dangerous things. People have jumped out of sixth floor windows while tripping because they believed they could fly!

One of the largest groups of drugs is known as 'stimulants'. These are drugs which make you feel 'high'. but although they make you feel energetic many people experience a strong sense of depression afterwards. The most common drugs in this group are speed pills or amphetamine sulphate. They are usually swallowed or sniffed but can be injected and it is injecting which causes most harm. Speed use is very common and it can be expensive. Users could be spending £50 or so a week if they take speed regularly. Someone who takes it rarely however by just swallowing the odd tablet could find it even cheaper than drinking beer – a tablet costs less than £1.

The expensive equivalent of speed is cocaine. Cocaine is usually sold by the gram and from it you can make a number of 'lines' of coke. These are sniffed – usually through a rolled up five pound note. A 'line' will cost about £15. It gives a sense of exhilaration when taken. But the effects of regular use can be equally as destructive as heroin.

Heroin is the drug we hear most about. It is produced from the fruit of the opium poppy. If you scratch the surface with a knife, resin seeps out. The product is a dirty brown raw opium traditionally smoked in a pipe. Not like the heroin most of us think about. That's because it is refined before arriving in Europe and the United States into a fine white powder.

Heroin is the most powerful pain killer known to man. In hospitals it is prescribed for patients with terminal illnesses such as cancer and offers them release from intense pain. Outside of hospitals you find heroin described under a wide variety of names – smack, skag, Helen, Horse, Harry and simply 'H'.

In the past heroin was injected. It gives a sudden 'rush' and a sense of feeling content and laid back. Today many people smoke heroin by 'chasing the dragon'; they use silver foil on which the powder is heated and a tube to 'chase' the smoke.

Heroin is cheap; one 'fix' will cost about £10. Sold as a

'lucky bag' or 'fold' at this price it is often very impure. Pushers make more money if they mix up or 'cut' the heroin with brickdust, talcum powder, Vim or another cheap white substance to make it go further. Like this heroin kills. You really don't know what you're taking – and if by chance you ever get *pure* heroin the risks of overdosing are great.

Heroin is one of a group of drugs called opiates. Many opiates manufactured synthetically are used for medical purposes, although they often find their way onto the illegal drug market as substitutes or alternatives to heroin. Most common amongst these is methadone. Although methadone is used to try and wean heroin addicts off heroin, many people have become addicted to methadone instead.

Until the mid seventies one of the biggest killers amongst drugs – not used for medical reasons – was the group known as barbiturates. Known by trade names like Seconal, Tuinal and Nembutal they are less commonly used nowadays but are still lethal when abused. It is very easy to overdose on these drugs and they can make you vulnerable to epileptic fits. All of these drugs are illegal substances and you can be prosecuted for possession of any of them. But there are groups of drugs which are not illegal to possess although their effects when abused are just as dangerous, if indeed not lethal.

Any substance that gives off vapour which has an intoxicating effect may be sniffed – from glues to petrol, nail varnish and typewriter correction fluid. They can be bought across the counter of any general store and are often on sale alongside childrens' sweets and toys. Butane aerosols are particularly dangerous: inhaled by a young person they produce an effect comparable to drunkenness – in excess the user can die.

Many doctors prescribe tranquillisers these days as a way of trying to help anxious or nervous patients cope with their problems. But tranquillisers can produce dependence and addiction and the long-term effects of taking these drugs can be very serious. Like all the drugs in this survey tranquillisers are abused.

Go into your local park, and you will probably be able to

find a special group of mushrooms known as 'magic mushrooms'. These are drugs. If you eat them they can produce mild hallucinations and yet it's quite legal to possess them. However it is illegal to 'prepare' them in any way; chop them up to make a soup and you've broken the law! They are dangerous too because unless you're an expert on fungi it is difficult to tell magic mushrooms from the poisonous or deadly varieties.

So much for the drugs themselves. But why do people start to take them? Why do some become hooked? And what happens once they have become hooked? To begin to answer those questions we turn to Melanie's story.

SECTION I

MELANIE'S STORY

Melanie's mother wrote to us: 'Thank God someone is trying to do something about drug addicts. My daughter is nineteen years old and is a heroin addict. Please send me a questionnaire and if you want to use my name I do not mind. I'll do anything to save someone else from becoming a drug addict.' We went to see Melanie and her mother and filmed them both for *Drugwatch*. Melanie wanted to say more than she was able to do in the programme. This is her story:

My name is Melanie, I am nineteen years old. I live in a bedsit, in a run-down part of London. I live alone and have done since I was sixteen, I do however have a little dog that we had since I was ten.

I'm unemployed just like four million others, what future does this 'system' have for me, – none. As far as eating goes, I make sure I have a cup of hot chocolate and a Topic daily. When I get my dole money I get a box of Ready-Brek and a loaf of bread, that will feed me for a week.

I'm a heroin addict, a registered one. I get four diamorphine ampules daily, which just keeps me 'straight'. Every morning I wake up sick, in a cold sweat and vomiting, I can't eat, drink or even smoke a cigarette until I've injected the first ampule. I pick up daily, some mornings I cannot even make it to the nearest toilet to do my fix so I have to use a phone box.

I feel that people must become more aware of this problem; for instance the word 'Junkie' – that word makes me sick, it's a label the media have branded on addicts. What springs to mind when you hear 'Junkie'? Well I think of a dirty, good-for-nothing scum. Someone that's classed in with muggers, rapists, murderers and such like, someone who'd

21

kill for drugs, in summary a very low form of life. I hate that word, it makes me sick. I'm a heroin addict. I'm still a person with feelings, hopes and pride, although that is slowly but surely being knocked out of me.

How can someone such as me get help, support and advice, when the system makes you so ashamed of yourself. I can't even tell my dearest friends. So I'm totally alone, ashamed of myself.

I expect you'd like to know how I became a heroin addict. It started when I left home, I was doing a two-year college course in computer programming, which I did despite the odds against me. I got my diploma. As I had my own flat, it became a hang-out for lots of others, who were a lot older than me and were already into drugs. Being young and naive I allowed them to use my place to fix. At first it disgusted me, frightened me, but after months of watching others apparently have a good time, I began to become curious.

My circumstances at this time began to go from bad to worse. I was refused social security as I was a student. I ate out of dustbins and walked on the streets looking for dogends that people had thrown away.

So I began taking speed as you don't need to eat on it. I'd tried dope and acid, but I wouldn't touch heroin as my 'friends' had told me it was addictive, so I believed it was alright to take sulphate. My circumstances got worse and worse and I began injecting sulphate as it made me feel I could cope, when really I was falling to pieces. All through the summer of 1983 I began fixing more and more sulphate. My landlord was trying to get me out and I came home one day to find my flat with the windows, frames, everything totally knocked out, my phone disconnected, my sink and shower totally ripped out and the water pipes cut off. As my flat was on the ground floor the three months that I lived in those conditions, I lived in constant fear. One evening I went out for an hour and a half, and when I returned my home had been totally ransacked. Everything was destroyed.

The 'friends' that had used my home to take their drugs and eventually got me to partake had by now left. Well, who wants to know someone who's unhappy? I quickly became anorexic and reached 5 stone 3lb. My mother and I weren't talking at the time. I was told she believed I was neglecting her.

I then took my first serious overdose. I sat in that hovel of a home for two days in total silence then took a large amount of barbiturates. The only reason I'm still alive is because I had so much sulphate in my system it saved my life.

It was not long after this that my mother moved to Hampshire and I moved to her old flat. This to me was an amazing break, a decent home, something to live for, so I began buying things to make it a home I could be proud of.

By this time, I had tried smack a few times, I used to burn it on foil. I liked it. It made me feel content and happy but I only took it occasionally as I was happy with my new home. I then got a job through an agency and was to start it on the Monday morning. However, late on Sunday night my electric blanket had gone wrong which caused a terrible fire. The flat was gutted. I lost everything, every bit of clothing I owned except the nightie I stood up in. I was devastated. I went in search of help and was sent from one office to another with no help from anyone. So after walking from one department to another, in nothing but a nightie and bare feet for three days, I realised I was going to receive no help.

I ended up in a squalid room robbed of all hope and faith in this so-called caring society. By now it had become rather trendy to take heroin, it was everywhere. There were so many places to buy it from you could even be choosy. In the hope of running away from my desperate unhappiness, loneliness and utter hopelessness I began taking heroin daily. When I was on it, it seemed to take away the terrible pain I was feeling, to such an extent I no longer felt anything. I began to need more and more to numb me as I knew I had a habit and had to feed it. I had to steal bars of chocolate for food, in desperation I went down to my GP. As I sat in that chair with my doctor watching me, I felt a terrible shame and fear of what his reaction would be, I respected him and hated myself. He asked me if I was taking any drugs, I burst into tears, tears of shame and hopelessness. He was however, very sympathetic and gave me a referral letter to take to a drug clinic.

I was feeling very desperate by now and thought that this drug clinic would help me and I'd be alright. The clinic is only open for drug patients on Mondays from 4 pm–6 pm so as it was a Monday, I believed at last I might get the help I desperately needed. When I arrived, I was coming down pretty badly but I knew that my GP had written me a good letter so I didn't see any problem. I was told to go to the second floor and report to the doctor's receptionist.

I stood at the desk and began to explain that I had been referred there by my GP. I don't think I'll ever forget the look she gave me as she realised I was a drug addict. She snatched the letter from me and while she opened it and read it she said in an icy voice 'I don't know why you've bothered. He won't see you, there's at least a five month waiting list for people like you.' She then said she'd keep the letter and a nurse would be in touch with me. I never heard from anyone.

As I left I broke into tears, thinking I'll be dead in five months, they don't want to help, they don't want to know. I was dumbfounded – I'd asked for help and was sent away with a flea in my ear. I couldn't go on, waking up every morning racking my brains trying to think of a way to get money to stop me being sick.

This is what led to maybe the biggest mistake of my life, I was at a dealer's house when this bloke turned up, he was a dope dealer. He offered to lay me on (give me credit) 1oz of blow (cannabis) to see if I could sell it. I always swore I'd never deal smack as I knew it was a destroyer, but blow does less damage than Valium and I do believe that, by itself, it is pretty harmless. So I began selling small amounts to friends, who smoked anyway. Heroin becomes an expensive 'hobby' when you have a habit, and once you've got a habit you no longer get that content, happy feeling off it, but you have to take it just to function. You don't make much money on selling blow to a few friends but I had no option. I'd tried to get help from the system and all that had done was make me feel suicidal. In the last year I had tried many times to end my life either by overdoses or cutting my wrists.

24

I'd been putting up one of my brother's mates for quite a few months by now, and through loneliness I began to care an awful lot for him although he was hated by everyone as he'd abused or ripped off everybody he'd ever met.

I kept him, fed him and loved him. One Saturday night around 6 pm my door was kicked in and within seconds eight plain clothed policemen were in my room. 'Freeze it's the drug squad.' I was arrested. It was only at that point that I realised just how serious what I'd done was, although I'd looked at it as just selling a bit of blow to friends.

It was through that bust that I got to see the doctor at the drug clinic, as my solicitor made the appointment. When I saw him I told him of the letter I'd brought up some five months earlier. He said he'd never seen it and that I should have been seen by him the day I went with my letter. He said the receptionist had no right to open his letters and called her in. She of course denied ever seeing me before and knew nothing of any letter, which made me look a liar.

So I got a script. The two weeks that followed I can only describe as hell. The guy I'd been living with had taken to beating me up, taking my script off me, even my food so I'd starve. He'd go for a few days then come back saying he loved me.

It got worse and worse. I was living in constant fear. I'd walk the streets and pray to God to please let me die. Then one Saturday he snatched all my drugs, (he also had a script by now) and he took the lot, overdosed. I called an ambulance. He got out of hospital that night, locked me in my room, viciously beat me and told me he was going to kill my dog, then me.

I did manage to escape from him after he'd broken my nose in two places. This was the reason for me going to my mother's and how she found out that I was a heroin addict. Within a week with my court case pending I was put into hospital for detoxification. I knew I wasn't ready but I did it for my mum.

After three days in hospital when the drugs began to wear off, I became suicidal. I cut my wrists again and could not stop crying. A nurse came to see me in hospital to tell me that they had taken me off too early so they gave me back my script. When my mum came to pick me up and was told, I could see the total disbelief in her eyes, as she thought that as long as my habit was gone I'd be alright.

My life went slowly downhill. I was prescribed more and more heroin and like a lamb to the slaughter I took it. From then on my life revolved around going to the chemist for my drugs. I wanted nothing else, just my fix.

So how did I wake up, you may wonder? When you're nineteen years of age and all you want to do is die, it doesn't take much to wake up. You see, I managed to get a week's script at once, which was an awful lot of heroin. I sat up one night dwelling on my life with all this gear and decided there were two choices: life or death. I chose life. Something inside me told me there was something worth living for. I hadn't found it yet but I knew it was there. So at 2 am that night I phoned City Roads, which helps people with drug problems. They told me to ring back the next morning to be assessed to see if I could go. After that phone call I prayed for the first time in ages. 'Please God let me live'. Sure enough the next day I was admitted.

That is where I met Rick, and we're going to be married soon. It's not been easy, but if you want something enough, *life*, then you fight for it and that's what Rick and I have been doing ever since we left City Roads.

Since Melanie wrote this, Joe her brother died from a drug overdose. Melanie was devasted and became deeply depressed. Tragically she turned to heroin to ease her pain. So once more Melanie is facing the struggle between life and heroin.

SECTION II

THE SURVEY

1. STARTING OFF

The first time I took heroin I was at my mum's house. My mum was messed up already on heroin and I asked her friend to inject me. She hesitated at first but after persuasion she did. I found it very sickly and didn't really like it. I was fourteen and a half at the time. It wasn't really what I had expected. Within a few weeks I was using it regularly. I used to get heroin mainly through my family and I used to take it at home. I used to spend about £280 a week on heroin which was obviously far more than I could ever afford.

I started breaking into houses for the money and eventually ended up threatening my mum and sister for what they had. I went out with a girl who was a prostitute and took money from her. I got into serious debt to the dealers – often they used to come looking for me. As a result of taking drugs I've been put in prison but that didn't stop me taking them because I was able to get them inside. Looking back I can see that I'd become a heroin addict within three months of first trying the stuff.

The boy who told us his story in the survey had started sniffing glue and other solvents when he was just eleven. His story is shocking. He started to take heroin so young and became addicted so quickly. But he isn't unusual.

How many people take drugs?
The people who took part in our survey had selected themselves. After an appeal on *That's Life* three thousand people wrote in to the programme offering to complete the

27

survey. But what percentage of the population do these three thousand people represent?

To answer that question we commissioned a national poll. About one thousand people were selected in various places up and down the country and stopped at random. They were asked whether they had ever tried illegal drugs, what they thought about drug-taking and for their views on drugs generally.

As a result of this independent poll we established that at least four million people have taken illegal drugs. That means nearly one in every ten people you know will have taken drugs.

The figure is staggeringly high. Of course the true figure is probably much higher still. We were asking people in the street to confess, after all, to having committed a crime: Think about it. If someone you didn't know came up to you in the street and asked you whether you had tried drugs, what would you be most likely to say? Most people would probably decide that it was better to say 'No, I've never even tried a drug.'

There are no official figures to verify this one. There is no obvious way of measuring illegal activity of course except by counting the people who get 'caught'. Figures tend to be based upon convictions, arrests, hospital admissions, addicts notified to the Home Office and so on. We do know that there has been an explosion in the amount of heroin seized in the past few years compared to seizure figures in the seventies. We also know that the number of new addicts notified to the Home Office increased by over five thousand in 1984. The figures on convictions for drug trafficking however have stayed virtually the same – so it would seem that the same number of people are being caught, dealing in ever-increasing quantities of drugs.

Which drugs do people take?

From our survey we can say that cannabis is the drug most people tried first and just about everyone in the survey had taken cannabis at some time. But nearly half the people in the survey had also tried heroin. Heroin is of course the drug we read so much about in the newspapers. However, the survey revealed that this focus on heroin hides a very serious threat from another drug – speed, or amphetamine sulphate.

Speed is a stimulant drug; it's not just a pep pill. The survey showed that eighty per cent of users had either tried or taken speed regularly. And like heroin it created massive problems for those who became addicted. We have cases of crime, illness and death amongst the regular speed users.

We heard a great deal about cocaine, too. The survey showed that few people try cocaine before they have used other drugs and only a small percentage were taking cocaine regularly.

In the following table we have listed the drugs which were most commonly mentioned in the drug user's survey and against these the percentage of people in the survey who are taking these drugs regularly now:

CANNABIS	69%
SPEED	30%
HEROIN	20%
TRANQUILLISERS	15%
METHADONE	11%
LSD	9%
COCAINE	6%

Table 1: Drugs taken most regularly now

The figures are slightly deceptive because the very large cannabis group at the top of the table includes those people who take drugs in addition to cannabis but who say that they *mostly* use cannabis. Only twenty-eight per cent of our sample smoke cannabis and take no other drugs. Most people then, who take drugs experiment with a number of different drugs. Nearly sixty per cent of people in our survey who are taking drugs now told us that they are taking more than one drug *regularly*.

Few people become regular users of the drug they first experiment with. Although as many as thirty per cent told us that the drug they take most regularly now is speed, only twelve per cent tried it as their first ever drug. And although twenty per cent told us that heroin was the drug they took most often now, only three per cent actually took heroin before they had used other drugs.

This table shows the first drug that users ever tried:

CANNABIS	59%
SPEED	12%
TRANQUILLISERS	6%
BARBITURATES	6%
LSD	5%
SOLVENTS	5%
HEROIN	3%
OTHER OPIATES	3%
MAGIC MUSHROOMS	1%

Table 2: First drug ever taken

When do they start?
One of the most alarming discoveries of the survey was that most people are younger than sixteen when they first try drugs. Sixty-two per cent are under sixteen when they first experiment. Some were under twelve when they started taking-drugs. Nearly four per cent, and twenty-seven per cent were between twelve and fourteen years old.

Under 12 years of age	4%
12–14 years	27%
14–16 years	31%
16–20 years	25%
21 or more years	13%

Table 3: Age when first tried drugs

From these figures we are able to say that drug abuse in Britain is a problem of the very young. Most people who try drugs are likely to be still at school; very few will be over the age of twenty-one when they first try drugs. These facts have mportant implications for prevention. As children experiment with drugs while they are still at school an effective education programme is needed whilst they are young enough for it to make an impact.

Is it just a big city problem?

Drug abuse is a national problem. It is not just concentrated in big cities. In our survey the respondents came from all over the country. It is certainly true to say that it is a greater problem in major urban areas; however it would be quite wrong to assume that the use of drugs is restricted to these areas.

We heard from cannabis users in almost every county of the United Kingdom. We discovered that speed use is also widespread. Second only to cannabis we found users not only in Britain's towns and cities but in many of the rural counties - Devon, Norfolk and the Highlands of Scotland. The use of heroin was spread right across the country; not just the major cities but also the rural areas, particularly in the south of England. Drug abuse is a nationwide problem.

Who uses drugs?

One of the striking features of the survey was how representative of every social class and various kinds of backgrounds the respondents seemed to be. They came from secure homes and broken homes, wealthy and poor backgrounds, educated and uneducated families, with employed and unemployed parents. A very high number of users were living at home with their families when they first tried drugs - seventy-two per cent. Only seven per cent were living alone at the time. So we can't say drug-taking is a direct result of poverty, or unemployment, or wealth and fast living. But we can turn to parents and say, if your child takes drugs he is likely to start when he is living at home with you.

Why do people first take drugs?

We have already seen that people first tend to experiment with drugs at a very young age. At fifteen years old on average. But some start much younger. One boy told us:

31

I started glue sniffing when I was about ten. My father was pretty well off. I thought it was very cool to go into a shop and get some. It was exciting. But then I went on to heroin, selling it to other twelve-year-olds. The drugs drastically affected my life, destroyed my education, my health, my relationship with my family. I ended up taking heroin, cannabis and LSD.

Fortunately he has now come off drugs and has stayed off for over nine months. Another boy told us about his first experience with drugs, aged eight:

It was a dare from a friend. We slipped into the senior school playground next door. My parents were getting divorced at the time and I didn't want to leave my dad. I'd just met my step-father and didn't like him. I'd heard that all your troubles leave you and I wanted to try it.

One fourteen-year-old boy was given heroin to try by his brother. He told us:

I was in the house with my brother and his girl. He was making up a fix and asked me if I wanted to try one. I wasn't sure at first but decided it would be okay, if I did it just once. It felt quite good. I didn't know what to expect. I'm not sure why I used it again. Probably because I knew all of my brother's friends were using it. I became addicted to heroin within four months.

One girl who was slightly older had been given the idea of taking speed because she thought it would help her lose weight. She told us:

My boyfriend had told me a lot about speed and said it was good and that I would lose weight if I took it because it removed your appetite. I very desperately wanted to be thin. So one day when he offered me some speed I accepted it. I took it and for a bit felt great. I wasn't hungry for a whole day. But I found that this was just a side-effect of the drug and it quickly brought all kinds of problems. I started to need it more and more often. I started to spend about £60 a week on speed – in fact I ended up using all the savings I had in the bank. I knew now that I had become addicted. I was only living half a life. Those days I couldn't get it were non-days. All I could do was just hang on until the next day when I could get some more. I just used to get very depressed and cry. Then I started over-eating – just the reason why I took speed in the first place. I couldn't talk to anyone. I couldn't smile anymore. Some days I couldn't even get up and get dressed. It was too much to handle.

Pathetic stories like this one were common in the survey. What emerges is that people first start taking drugs as a social activity. Indeed it is most often pressure from friends which first spurs them on to try drugs.

One girl from the Midlands who was just fourteen when she started using drugs told us:

I was in a group of four or five people, all of them using drugs. I was called 'chicken' a few times; they were joking about my refusal to smoke. We were watching television. By the time the programme had finished they'd persuaded me to smoke two joints. My advice to other people would be, remember that when someone passes you a joint or a pill or whatever, they're actually saying 'let me spoil your life'.

She ended up on a mixture of cannabis and speed. Fortunately she has now given up taking drugs altogether but looking back she believes 'they prevented me making any effort to go on with my education or finding work'.

Pressure from friends is the keynote – the reason why so many young people experiment with drugs. One girl told us:

My mother was a schoolteacher and my father worked for the Council. I joined a gang in our city and when I was nine a friend of mine gave me some Valium he'd stolen from his parents. I took it to make me feel important so that I wouldn't feel afraid of running riot. I went on to take heroin after that and used to pay for it by prostitution. I

33

got my heroin from a pimp. It was my payment for working for him. I got a limitless supply if I pleased the customers and worked hard for him. If not he withheld the supplies.

This girl came from a very secure and comfortable home – it seems almost incredible that she could reach such depths of misery. The pressure from friends to try drugs is enormous. One boy who started on cannabis told us:

Everyone else was doing it and I felt left out, so I thought why not.

Drugs are rarely forced on people by evil pushers and peddlers. It's pressure perhaps of a more insidious kind – pressure to be 'like everyone else'.

We heard this with monotonous regularity from users in our survey when we asked them why they had started drug-taking:

I was part of a group of friends, many of whom took drugs so I started smoking on a social basis.

I wanted to try some dope because my friends were smoking it. At first I didn't really feel anything but everyone else liked it so I thought there must be something in it and tried it again.

I didn't want to feel a chicken and my friends kept telling me I was because I wouldn't try any dope.

And when we asked people to say from whom they first obtained their drugs most told us that their friends had been their first suppliers.

Friends	74%
Family	5%
Dealer (who was not a friend)	10%
Doctor	9%
Stranger	2%

Table 4: Who supplied the first drugs

So the reason most young people first try drugs is because they are reacting to pressure from their friends. You might think, well of course that's true for drugs like cannabis but it can't be the case for something like heroin. No real friend would start you off on heroin. But we found even with hard drugs like heroin and cocaine that friends were the source of the first drugs used.

DRUG	FRIEND	FAMILY	DEALER
Heroin	64%	8%	28%
Speed	76%	3%	19%
Cannabis	83%	6%	10%
Cocaine	85%		

Table 5: Who supplied first drug according to drug supplied

And when we asked where users obtained their drugs only thirteen per cent told us they got them 'on the street'. Nearly forty per cent got them in someone's house, the rest got them at school, at discos and parties.

Why do young people take drugs so readily in the company of friends? Clearly drug-taking itself is an enjoyable experience, initially at least. Coupled with that there is the excitement of behaving in an illicit and rebellious way. Drugs, it seems, make young people feel grown up and rebellious at the same time. Whilst our users' parents might have gone behind the bike sheds at school to smoke a Woodbine, they will sniff glue, roll a joint or chase the dragon.

Young people know little about the drugs they're trying. We asked users to tell us what they thought about drug-taking before they actually started taking drugs. Their answers fell into three categories. Just over a third thought about drugs in a negative way. Another third thought drugs might actually have a positive effect on their lives, the rest knew nothing about their effects at all.

So what conclusions can we draw then about 'starting off'

on drugs? Most people will experiment because of pressure from friends. We can reject all the ideas of children being seduced into taking drugs by evil pushers standing on street corners, waiting to tempt young people. The danger doesn't come from strangers but from friends. It usually happens in the home and with friends of the same age.

Reading this book now you may feel that this pressure, whilst a threat to many people, won't effect you or your family or friends. Think again. Peer pressure, as it's called by sociologists, is a remarkably powerful force.

We conducted an experiment to see just how powerful peer pressure can be. We asked a group of teenagers to take part in the experiment with sociologist, Professor Laurie Taylor. Professor Taylor explained to the young people who were to be our stooges that he would ask them to count a number of beats on a metronome. But when he gave a secret signal – rubbing his nose – stooge number one should count either one more or one less beat than the number of beats he had actually heard. The rest should give the same answer.

At this point a fifth teenager, the 'subject', unaware that the four stooges had been briefed, was invited to sit at the end of the line. The experiment was explained again to the group but this time Professor Taylor did not repeat the information about the deliberate mistake and the secret signal.

The experiment now began. Professor Taylor started the metronome and let it tick up to twenty times. He rubbed his nose in one in every five or so trials. Nine times out of ten the subject followed suit with the incorrect answer given. We repeated the experiment with five different subjects. They all conformed. Afterwards we asked them if they knew they were giving us the wrong answer. One told us:

I thought that I'd missed one or counted one too many or something and I wasn't sure what was right so I just did what the others did. Sometimes I thought twice and felt like saying the number I'd counted but then I felt stupid and didn't dare say what I really thought.

Another said:

> If you say a different number to your friends then you feel
> stupid. You think perhaps you are wrong and they're right
> and you don't want to be the odd one out.

The experiment illustrates the extraordinary power of peer
pressure, and it always works. It has been carried out with
people of all ages and they behave in exactly the same way.
Even mathematics professors! Asked to do simple additions
and multiplications the results were the same as for the
children. People conform more often than not to what their
peers say. It's easier. If the pressure is to take drugs then the
reaction is just the same. It's easier to say yes and be like all
your friends than say no and be the odd one out and feel
stupid.

Another lesson we should learn is that as users seemed to
know so little about drugs before taking them, there clearly is
a need for more education about drugs and what they do to
you. Furthermore, children need this information about
drugs when they're young. By the time they're sixteen it is
often too late.

From the survey it is clear that people who go on to try
drugs like heroin tend to be those people who started taking
drugs very young. Those who start later tend to be less likely
to go on to take harder drugs. They seem to be much more in
control of their habit. Young people – adolescents – are
much less able to cope and control their drug-taking so it
seems particularly important to hold them back from
experimenting with any kind of drugs. It is important to give
them a chance to grow up a bit, a chance to enjoy other things
in life.

GETTING HOOKED

Grey, Grey
No one ever listens to a word you say,
But you'd be mugs
To take drugs.
Drugs just help you fade away,
Drugs desert you,
Friends desert you,
The people you love
Have to watch you pay.

Use your head – don't dare,
Drugs can't match imagination.
It's a cold spear,
And beware,
It's only going to cause complication.

If you don't do,
It's up to you,
You don't have to waste your money.
It's your life – choose life
And drugs aren't in it,
Drugs aren't in it.
Choose Life, not drugs.

(From Scottish Office
Drugs Prevention Campaign)

So far we've looked at the reasons why young people start to take drugs. But what happens to these young people if they carry on taking drugs – experimenting perhaps with different kinds of drugs? What happens when they start to depend on drugs, when they start *needing* to get high, and realising that they need more drugs to get the same effect?

One girl who is now twenty-three started taking cannabis and speed when she was fourteen, living in a children's home in London. Two years later she was offered heroin at a friend's flat:

> The first time I fixed heroin I was sixteen. Somebody else fixed me – it wasn't as painful as I thought it would be. But I was violently sick. Then I felt even more sick and I can remember thinking why do people do this if it just makes you feel sick?

She didn't think she'd take heroin again after that experience. But then a friend told her she wouldn't be sick the next time. It only happens, they told her, the first time:

> My problem was that I'd been smoking dope for some time and I found it didn't have any real effect on me anymore. I wanted something to give me that feeling. So when they told me I would not feel sick on heroin the next time and that it would make me feel good I thought I'd try it again.

So she started to fix heroin regularly. After just a couple of months she discovered she could not manage without heroin. Seven years later, how does she feel?

> I'm still taking all kinds of drugs, including heroin. I've tried to give up but I can't. Drugs have made me more lonely and unhappy although I originally thought they would make me feel happier and less lonely. I've had a lot more bad luck since being involved with drugs. I've turned to prostitution to pay for my drugs which at times costs me about two hundred pounds a week. I've had to stop the prostitution now because I've been raped twice. The last time I ended up getting pregnant and had to have an abortion. There's no doubt in my mind that both rapes happened because of taking drugs.

Most of my friends are dead – one of them was my lover and another my best friend. I've had a string of broken relationships and friendships. Nobody trusts me. My health is awful – I've had hepatitis twice. My liver is in a terrible state. I don't want to die. People are so scared of me – no one will get close to me. Drugs have made me very unhappy. I regret ever getting on to them.

A story that's not uncommon in our survey. Most people who become addicted to drugs like heroin suffer considerably as a result. But there is a difference between the drugs people take, how involved with the drugs they become and the way it affects their lives.

There is little doubt that many hundreds of thousands of people try drugs and experience few problems. Most of us know someone who has tried cannabis or may ourselves have tried it and not ended up in desperate straits. Indeed we may have enjoyed the experience.

In our survey we had a small number of people who had only ever taken cannabis and no other drugs – just twenty-four people out of more than one thousand drug users. However it was this group who told us they suffered least as a consequence of taking drugs, indeed many said that taking cannabis had positive effects.

We asked users how drug-taking had affected their lives, and we classified their answers into positive and negative effects:

Drug	Negative effects	Positive effects
Cannabis only	25%	63%
Cannabis and other drugs	41%	59%
Speed	77%	18%
Heroin	91%	6%

Table 6: Effects of drugs on user's life

Overall about one in five people in the survey told us that drug-taking had had no ill effects on their lives and some of them told us that taking drugs had been beneficial. But clearly the majority who took speed or heroin regularly have a different story to tell. Their message is clear and very distressing, as we will show later in this chapter.

Most of the group who only tried cannabis told us that they didn't feel addicted, that they hadn't got mixed up in any crime as a result of their drug-taking and that they had no health problems subsequently. But there were some stories which demonstrated that smoking cannabis regularly can create serious problems. One man who is married with two young children and is unemployed told us:

> I spend fifteen pounds a week from our social security on cannabis. I know it's a terrible strain on my wife. I feel very guilty, as though I'm carrying a great weight on my shoulders. I know that I should be buying things that we need with the money. It stops me getting on with my life, which I want to do. I worry about my health because I've become very moody and seem to neglect myself. Thank God my wife sticks by me and tries to understand. The only advice I can give to other people is 'don't start'.

His story was unusual amongst this group of people who use cannabis but have never got mixed up with any other drugs. Not surprisingly they suffer far less than those who take drugs like heroin or cocaine regularly.

A very practical piece of advice came from one cannabis user who told us:

> I believe cannabis is about as safe as alcohol. I've experienced cannabis as a user and alcohol as a publican's son. Don't ever mix cannabis with alcohol and don't drive while under the influence of cannabis. Be careful where and who you take drugs with. Never take anything harder than cannabis or see people who regularly do.

People can start their drug-taking with cannabis – and never progress to other drugs. To try and understand why this group seems to experience fewer or sometimes no problems we compared them with those groups who took other drugs. The major difference was that the 'cannabis only' group started taking drugs later, on average aged nineteen, than the hard drugs users, who were experimenting at fifteen years old whilst they were still at school.

So if you delay the initiation you can perhaps reduce the chance of someone turning into a problem user. Of course, there are always risks. However, it is clear that the age at which you start to take drugs and what drugs you take will determine the problems you are likely to encounter. The problem for many people is that once they've started to use cannabis regularly they go on to take other drugs. Most people in the survey fall into this category.

Which drugs do regular users take?

We asked people to tell us which drug they were using most regularly. You will see that the 'cannabis only' group, as we said before, is very small. However there is a large group which we have called 'cannabis plus'. These are people who told us that they took cannabis most regularly but they admitted to using other drugs regularly as well.

Cannabis only	3%
Cannabis plus other drugs	32%
Heroin	26%
Speed	13%
LSD	5%
Tranquillisers	5%
Cocaine	3%
Other opiates	6%

Table 7: Drugs taken *most* regularly

Of those who fell into the 'cannabis plus' group we asked them to tell us which other drugs they used most regularly. They told us:

Speed and other stimulants	65%
LSD and other hallucinogens	44%
Heroin and other opiates	13%
Tranquillisers and other sedatives	4%

Table 8: Drugs taken by regular 'cannabis plus' users

As can be seen, speed and other stimulants were the most popular other drugs used by cannabis users, after that came LSD and some took heroin or another kind of opiate.

Who supplies drugs?

We thought it might be interesting to discover whether there was any difference between the answers people gave to the question, 'Where did you *first* get the drug from?' and 'From where did you get this drug once you were using it regularly?' We divided it into three categories; friends, family or dealers:

DRUG	FRIEND		FAMILY		DEALER	
	first	sub-sequently	first	sub-sequently	first	sub-sequently
Heroin	73%	41%	2%	—	26%	69%
Speed	66%	58%	2%	—	33%	60%
Cannabis	88%	75%	4%	—	4%	29%

Table 9: Comparison of where drugs are obtained by
          regular users

(The figures do not add up to one hundred per cent because some people obtain their drugs from more than one source on a regular basis.)

In nearly all cases it is the user's friends who first supply the drug the user most regularly takes. However the dealer soon begins to supply the user.

One girl who started on cannabis, shortly went on to take LSD. She told us:

> For five years I wasted my life. I failed my exams, I lost friends and made enemies. I became withdrawn and frightened. My family were very distressed. I attempted suicide and was given hospital treatment which was very helpful. My GP was terrific in helping me. But the main problem is staying off drugs. You have to change your whole lifestyle and most of your friends to stay out of temptation's way.

Another young man who became addicted to methadone after taking a number of different drugs told us:

> While I was on the drug I was calm. But as soon as I came down anyone who spoke to me was in danger of getting hit with anything I could find. I started very young when I was just nine. At school they didn't teach us anything about drugs, they just said 'stay away from them.' That just made me inquisitive. But looking back now I've got one very important piece of advice – stay away from the hard drugs like heroin.

The survey bears out his advice very clearly. Once you move on to hard drugs your whole life seems to change. If you look back to Table 6 you can see that ninety-one per cent of those who took heroin regularly said that they believe the drug has had a negative effect on their lives.

Do drugs lead to crime?
Of course possession of most of these drugs is in itself a crime. Four out of five regular heroin users told us that they had criminal convictions for crimes they had committed since taking drugs. Crimes like burglary, shoplifting, supplying drugs and possession of drugs. We even had one case of attempted murder:

> I started taking drugs when I was just eleven, smoking

cannabis. I went on to taking speed. One day when I was coming off speed I was offered a shot of heroin. It was wonderful. It helped me to mellow out and I felt less angry with the world. So I started taking more and from then I was using it regularly. To start with I didn't have to pay for it because I was going out with a girl who was a nurse and she used to get it from her work for free for me. But we broke up and I moved away. I became so desperate to supply my habit that I got involved in an armed robbery when I held up a chemist's shop. I was caught and charged with attempted murder and armed robbery. I'm now in prison.

Not surprisingly it is the heroin users who get into most trouble:

Convictions	heroin users	speed users	cannabis/plus users
Possession	53%	27%	20%
Burglary/Theft	43%	22%	16%
Shop-Lifting	13%	11%	7%
Suppling Drugs	15%	8%	–
Assault	13%	7%	7%
Prostitution	4%	–	–
None	20%	52%	63%

Table 10: Convictions since taking drugs

Few people who take heroin regularly, just one in five, had not got into trouble with the police. We wanted to know if this was as a direct result of their drug-taking and asked users to tell us if they had been in trouble before taking drugs. Nearly all the cannabis and cannabis plus users told us that they had had a virtually trouble-free background. But one in four of the speed and heroin users had been in trouble with the police before they started using drugs. However once drugs crept into their lives this figure jumped alarmingly.

More than half the speed users and most herion users had criminal convictions. Drugs clearly lead to crime.

The heroin users told us that nearly all these crimes were caused by their drug-taking. The speed users told us that more than two thirds of their crimes were a result of drug-taking. So what made them turn to crime?

The answer is obvious. Heroin, speed and cocaine – are expensive habits. One girl told us:

I spent two to three hundred pounds a week on heroin. Of course I couldn't afford it so I turned to crime. Once I burgled a chemist's shop for drugs, other times I would steal to get the money. I've been in prison for assault because I'd got very stoned once and started fighting in the street. My husband borrowed some money to buy a new car – I spent the money on heroin as soon as he got it. I got through that three thousand pounds in less than three months.

Another girl told us about the crime she became involved with once she'd become addicted to heroin:

At first I could afford it because I used less and was only spending about one hundred to two hundred pounds a week. But as I got used to the drug I found I needed it more and more. It became difficult to pay for heroin. I ended up going to Iran with my husband to organise a drugs deal. We were caught and I was sent back to Britain. As soon as I arrived at the airport I was arrested. The loan companies to whom I owed so much money were waiting for me. I ended up in prison.

In fact nearly half the heroin users have served a prison sentence since taking heroin; nearly a quarter of speed users, too, have spent time in prison.

The cost of drugs

Drugs cost a great deal of money and some drug users get into serious debt. One young man who is a heroin addict told us:

> I need to find about four to five hundred pounds a week to pay for my heroin. I've got a job but of course I don't earn this kind of money. So I get the extra by burglary, theft or shoplifting. Sometimes I turn to prostitution. I can't keep up any of my financial commitments as an addict. I spend everything I get on drugs.

Another man told us:

> I spent about three hundred and fifty pounds a week on heroin. I had to steal or do anything to pay the cost of my habit. Once I persuaded my bank that I was starting up a business and they gave me an overdraft of seven thousand pounds. I was always in debt. I had a house worth forty-three thousand pounds. I had to sell it to pay off my debts for heroin.

It seems that once you're really hooked you don't care about how you pay for your habit. One girl told us about her cocaine habit:

> I could easily spend more than a hundred and fifty pounds a day on coke. I was completely addicted to it. But it wasn't of the slightest importance how much it cost. I just used to borrow and borrow, more and more. Even if I couldn't have borrowed I would have got the money somehow. I would have stolen or sold my body. When I went into treatment a year ago I was twenty-five thousand pounds in debt. My life was completely unmanageable.

So how expensive is drug-taking if you're a regular user? Our users told us how much they spent on average a week on their habit:

Drug	nil	£ 1-10	£ 10-20	£ 20-30	£ 30-70	£ 70-200	£ 200-250	£ 250+
Cannabis	20%	30%	21%	8%	–	–	–	–
Cannabis plus	64%				15%	5%	–	–
Speed	29%				33%	27%	8%	3%
Heroin	7%				8%	31%	10%	39%

Table 11: Average weekly expenditure on drugs

For nearly all the heroin users this was more than they could afford. For two thirds of the speed users it was more than they could afford. Of those who were taking cannabis plus other drugs nearly one third told us they could not afford their habit and one in five of those just taking cannabis told us that their habit was too expensive for their pocket. It is not surprising then that someone gripped by addiction and without the means to support their habit will turn to crime.

One family we talked to has first-hand experience of crime. Mark was a heroin addict and when we spoke to his parents and sister he was serving a prison sentence for burglary. When his father first wrote to us he said:

A drug addict like my son becomes a stranger in your own home. The child you thought you could control can change into a monster. I speak from experience. And yet my wife and I still love our son.

When we went to see Mr Valentine he told us about the torment the family suffered, the torment that continues while Mark is in prison. Twice Mark had violently attacked his father. Mr Valentine told us:

The second time my son attacked me was awful. It took my wife, my son-in-law and my daughter to hold him off.

The strength produced by these drugs is incredible. I knew then that the next time it happened I would have to think about survival. I know this may sound terrible, but I planned how I could kill my son if he attacked me again when my wife was around. The whole thing then became a nightmare. In the end I had to have treatment for it. Then one night I was sitting with my wife and I told her what I'd planned in my mind. I told her how if he attacked me again it would be either him or me. Then my dear wife got up and walked over to a drawer. She opened it and pulled out a huge lump of stone and she said the next time he gets you on the floor, I'll kill him with this stone. It's hard to see now how three normal people, me, my wife and my son could end up like this but that is what drugs can do.

Mark's sister told us:

It's so hard because I love Mark. I feel for him. But there are two Marks. The Mark who's my brother, the one I love dearly. Then there's this other Mark, I don't love him – I hate him for the hurt and the upset he's brought to the whole family.

How drugs change your life

I started mixing with a new crowd of people and they were all using heroin. My boyfriend was using it and I tried to get him to stop. He didn't, and stupidly I thought if you can't beat them, join them. But I found that it was a very expensive habit. Even if I had a job paying a thousand pounds a week, I still couldn't have afforded it because the more money you've got, the more skag you buy. I must have stolen and borrowed over a thousand pounds from my family and the same again from my friends to pay for my heroin. Eventually I got caught stealing and was sent to prison. There I got off drugs. To anyone thinking of trying I'd say don't do it! It turns you into a liar, a thief. You lose all sense of self-respect and feeling. And you die a little bit every day you're on drugs.

One girl, a heroin addict told us:

> I'm no longer a healthy person. My body can't function without heroin. I've lost all the respect my family once had for me. Now I don't give a damn about my life.

Another girl who started with Valium when she was fourteen and now at twenty-eight takes any kind of drug she can get her hands on told us:

> My foster parents have disowned me. I've got terrible arthritis in my legs, feet and shoulder. I've got over two hundred scars on my arms and legs from needles.

Another drug addict told us:

> I couldn't work I was so stoned. I've been in hospital loads of times for overdoses. I've had three marriages and none of them have worked because of drugs.

A lot of drug users identified serious problems arising from their graduation to hard drugs. One girl who started on LSD when she was only eleven told us:

> It was only once I'd got on to heroin and left school that my life really changed. I found I couldn't hold down a job for more than a few months. My family suffered terribly – they never knew what state or mood I would be in. I was forever suffering from colds and other ailments which I know were drug related.

Another girl who injected speed told us:

> Taking drugs nearly killed me. I lost everything I ever possessed and became a no one. My husband abused me violently. I became a very nasty person. I almost destroyed my mother and I know I wrecked her second marriage. I went to prison twice. My health was absolutely dreadful. I was dirty, messy, untidy, became broke and eventually

homeless. In short I was a complete mess and worse, there were times when I felt I could kill those I love most, my mother and my brother.

She has given up drugs and has settled down with a job and is now happily married.

A lot of regular users suffer from poor health. They neglect themselves, stop eating properly and therefore have less resistance to infections. Regular use of dirty syringes, of course, is likely to result in problems. Although most people who manage to give up drugs make full recoveries from their health problems, some are not so fortunate. One girl who took heroin told us:

> I got hepatitis from using dirty needles with the result I now have a weak liver.

And for some the consequences extend beyond their own damaged health. One girl who started taking drugs when she was given tranquillisers at the age of nine and ended up taking heroin, told us:

> I'd been working the streets for a few years and when I was fourteen I got pregnant. My son was born deaf and with spinal injury. I know that this was due to my drug-taking and the consequences of getting VD from prostitution which was the only way I could pay for my habit.

A terrible story. Her son has been adopted now because she was unable to cope. Of course it need never have happened. She became a prostitute because it was the only way a girl of fourteen could pay for a habit that costs hundreds of pounds a week. But why do people take drugs that ruin their lives, risk their physical health and the lives of their families and friends? The answer of course is addiction.

Drugs and Addiction

The very words 'addiction' and 'addict' seem to be synonymous with drug abuse. But what is addiction? Do all people who take drugs become addicts? Do they have to take drugs regularly to become an addict? Or is an addict simply someone who takes drugs regularly?

We asked the users in our survey to tell us whether they were addicted to the drug they were taking most regularly.

DRUG	FELT ADDICTED
Heroin	95%
Cocaine	83%
Speed	70%
Cannabis Plus	24%
Cannabis	13%

Table 12: Drugs and addiction

In this 'league of addictiveness' it would seem that if you take heroin regularly then you are almost certain to feel addicted. The same seems to be true for cocaine and seven out of ten of the speed users also felt they had become addicted. However there is a striking difference between these groups and those who use cannabis. Only one in four of the cannabis plus group and only about one in ten of those who take cannabis told us they felt addicted to it.

It used to be said that cannabis was non-addictive. And speed and cocaine, it was thought, could not create addicts as such because users were not supposed to experience physical withdrawal symptoms. Addiction has always been defined in terms of physical symptoms. But we asked users what *they* meant by addiction.

We asked them to describe what they thought made them feel addicted. One girl who used cannabis regularly told us:

The craving for a smoke during lessons at school. Not being able to function first thing in the morning without a smoke. Loss of weight and appetite. Disrupted sleep patterns. Nausea.

She was just fourteen and a half when she began to feel

52

unable to function without using cannabis. Another boy told us why he felt addicted to cannabis at the age of twelve:

I was getting really ratty with people over stupid things because of the drug. When I was on it I was calm but as I came down off it anyone who said anything to me was in danger of getting hit with the first thing I could find.

Obviously many people take cannabis and don't experience these sort of feelings. But with drugs like speed people are much more likely to experience problems. One speed user told us:

If I couldn't get any amphetamines I used to get into a terrible depression. I couldn't function. I would just sit there or lie down. I needed speed more and more to enable me to function at all. I needed more by the day. In the end I couldn't eat, sleep or do anything at all until I'd had at least a gram of speed and I needed that at least three or four times a day.

Of course we expect to hear horrific stories of the painful withdrawal experienced by heroin users – but how do they discover they're addicted? One heroin user explained how she found out that she was hooked:

I knew I had become addicted when I woke up one morning and started vomiting yellow bile. It was really painful. I was sweating and yet at the same time I was freezing. Then I got diarrhoea. I was in agony. As soon as I scored and got that hit I felt fine and all the illness went away.

Another heroin user wrote:

I was fourteen and had been taking heroin for about three months after some sixth formers offered it to me in the toilets at school. I suddenly started to be physically ill if I couldn't get it any day. I would wake up in the morning, sweating, shaking, sometimes even vomiting. It wasn't until I'd got some smack a few hours later that these withdrawal symptoms would go away and I felt fine again.

So, it's when you can't get the drug and you feel you can't cope without it, that you know you're hooked – and what is frightening is that it doesn't seem to take very long before that happens. About one third of speed users felt addicted within three months of first taking the drug, whilst half the heroin and cocaine users felt addicted within the same period. One cocaine addict told us:

I became addicted to cocaine after about three months. Whenever I couldn't get it I would be moody and aggressive, I would shake violently and become weak. Sometimes I would vomit. But the moment I got a dose of coke all these symptoms seemed to vanish. Coke became as vital to me as air for breathing.

We expect drugs like heroin to create addiction. But why do some users feel addicted to supposedly non-addictive drugs? One of the most respected experts in this field, Dr John Strang, runs a Drugs Dependency Unit near Manchester. He told us there is no doubt that with many drugs there is a very real *physical* dependence. When someone has been taking drugs on a regular basis their body gets used to the presence of the drug. But when the drug is suddenly taken away they develop a real physical illness that is brought on by stopping the drugs.

However in addition to this is the drug user's reason for taking drugs in the first place, his *need* to take the drugs and this need does not necessarily disappear when he gives up. In other words it is possible to be addicted to a drug which doesn't necessarily involve physical withdrawal. Take cocaine for example. With this drug most people who feel unable to function without cocaine also suffer very few, if any, physical withdrawal symptoms. However there is no doubt whatsoever that people do become extremely dependent on coke.

It is calculated that some twelve million people use the drug regularly. In America cocaine is a huge problem. Just outside New York at Fairoaks, New Jersey, a special clinic has been set up for cocaine addicts – people who can't break the habit and many who have been ruined by it. Through the clinic's doors every day come lawyers, business men, doctors, actors – people who can afford its fees from just about every walk of life.

One man we talked to was the President of a large company making pharmaceutical products. He squandered two and a half million dollars on cocaine! He told us:

I was at a party in a doctor's flat. He asked me if I wanted to try some coke. He said it was great. First of all I said no thank you. Then I decided to try just one line. After that they had to practically tear me away from it. I had to go out and buy some straightaway because I liked it so much. So I went on taking it, eventually spending millions of dollars on cocaine because I needed it so much.

He ended up receiving special treatment at the clinic. For what had been thought to be a non-addictive drug he suffered severe physical and psychological damage:

My nose – the septum – is totally burned away. In fact you can pass a dime from one side to the other. I can remember when it started to break through because I had to do massive amounts of coke to stop the pain. Then when the bleeding started I would jump in the shower and leave it on for up to two hours to help stop the bleeding. And then I'd have to shove cotton wool up my nose every once in a while when I wanted to go out on the road. Then driving along the highway I would be pulling the cotton out of my nose, snorting coke and then putting cotton back up my nose. It was a horror show.

Of course the range of drugs and substances to which the problems of addiction apply is far wider than just heroin and cocaine. Drugs, like tranquillisers, cigarettes and alcohol are

55

very much part of this group. The difference is they are socially acceptable drugs. But the alcoholic experiences just as painful withdrawal symptoms – and look at the experiences of nicotine addicts who try to kick the weed! There is a very strong need to understand addiction beyond the ideas of physical withdrawal. Much of the concern raised in the survey touches the social and emotional problems in people's lives. And it's important to see how all these problems don't just apply to illegal drugs and those obtained illegally. One man who took part in the survey told us about his addiction which began after he was prescribed Valium by his doctor when he was just twenty-one. He's now forty-one. He told us:

I blame my doctor for why I started. I went to see him because I felt depressed and unwell. He prescribed Valium. To start with I felt very good. I'd always been someone who spoke out against drug-taking. But now twenty years later people call me names and don't like talking to me or have anything to do with me.

After I'd been taking Valium for a bit I tried to stop. But I felt shaky and very bad. I went back to the doctor but he just gave me more. Then I started taking hash too.

At the time I had a wife and children to support. We're divorced now because she's had more than she can take. My children don't want much to do with me even though they're now nearly all grown up.

Looking back I became addicted within about four months. When I had none left I used to start panicking and getting into a very bad mood and taking it out on my wife and family. If I couldn't get my pills I would do anything to try and calm myself down. Sometimes the experiments went wrong and I ended up in hospital.

I've had convictions for shoplifting, burglary, assault and some for being drunk and disorderly. Before I took drugs I'd never been in trouble.

I've taken many overdoses – in fact I've been in hospital fifteen times for overdosing. But as soon as I wake up I start taking them again. I always carry a spare bottle and the staff in hospital don't know I've got it so it's easy to start again.

I've tried to give up but the help I've had hasn't been any good. Talking alone doesn't help. As soon as I get out of hospital treatment I start again. The only time I've managed to stop taking pills for more than a few months was when I was in prison although I was able to get them in prison when I wanted to start again.

My health is now terrible. I can't get a job and anyway even if I could I wouldn't be able to do it now. My only advice to anyone thinking of trying drugs is don't start, because once you do there's no stopping.

Well, that's surely part of the answer. If you don't start you can't get hooked. Clearly not all users who start taking drugs become addicted. How can someone ensure that experimenting with drugs does not end up disastrously? The answer is they can't. The reasons why one person will become an addict and another will be able to control his drug-taking are not known. We can't isolate the reasons why some people get hooked and provide a checklist for identifying those people most 'at risk'. All we can say is that if you start taking drugs there is no guarantee that you won't end up an addict.

3. KICKING THE HABIT

When friends told Kate smoking heroin would make her feel good, they forgot to tell her something else – how bad it would also make her feel; how she'd start to look tired, spotty, and unhealthy; how she'd lose her friends, her looks and her interest in everything but heroin; how she'd soon have to take heroin, not to get high but just to stop feeling down; how she'd eventually first risk blood disease, liver damage, even heart failure.

(From the Government's 'Anti-Heroin Campaign'.)

For many people 'drug addiction' sounds like a terminal illness, which is inevitably fatal. This of course is quite untrue – and in itself very counterproductive. If you are hooked and believe that there's no hope, then in turn the chances of kicking a habit are slim. Similarly if you believe withdrawal will be so agonising that you simply won't be able to cope you're less likely to give it a try. So there are two myths that make giving up drugs even more difficult than it would otherwise be; the myth that a habit will never be overcome and the myth that withdrawal will be so painful that any attempt to give up will be doomed to failure.

The survey has some very good news. Firstly, a great many addicts *do* kick the habit. Just under half the drug users in our survey told us that they were no longer taking drugs. Almost half the regular users of speed and half the heroin users managed to come off all drugs and are still off. The message is encouraging – you can give up drugs no matter how dependent you may have become.

How do people who come off drugs manage to kick their

habit? Most, surprisingly, manage on their own, that is without treatment. Others do have treatment. We asked people to tell us how, if they had stopped taking drugs for more than three months, they had succeeded:

On your own (without treatment)	70%
Following a recognised form of treatment	19%
Whilst in prison	16%

Table 13: How people give up drugs

The most successful group seem to be those drug users who give up without specialist help. Just over a third of this group managed to stay off altogether; the rest drifted back to drug-taking. Similarly, of those who gave up following a recognised form of treatment, just over a third managed to stay off completely – two thirds have drifted back. And of those who gave up in prison just under a third have managed to stay off since giving up – the rest of this group have also drifted back. So what the survey shows is that it can be done, and can be done as effectively *without* treatment as with it. Treatment usually involves some form of pain relief to deal with the symptoms of withdrawal during the first few days of what is known as 'detoxification'. But since most people choose to do it without that help, there goes that other myth – that withdrawal is so acutely painful that the addict is bound to relapse. The survey shows that during the early days when the drug user experiences withdrawal symptoms he does manage to withstand the temptation to take drugs. But the difficulty is staying off drugs permanently once the hard work of detoxification is completed. And it's here as well as in the early stages that a drug user needs support and help from other people, from his family and friends.

Can your family help?
Nearly two thirds of the people in our survey did not ask for help from their families or close friends. It seems that many people feel that they can't talk about drugs or their drug

problem and are afraid of how their families are going to react. One boy who started taking drugs when he was thirteen told us:

> I became a heroin addict very quickly. I wanted help to come off, especially because I was so young. It had been a taboo subject in our family so I couldn't ask them for help. I couldn't go to them until I was expelled from school for taking drugs. I was fifteen.

Had his family been more supportive, he told us, he felt he might have been able to deal with his problem before it resulted in his expulsion from school.

One girl who was sniffing glue when she was just nine years old told us how, as a teenager, she became addicted to the opiate drug known as poppy milk.

> I tried to reach out to my mum and dad but they just couldn't grasp it. I can't and I don't blame them. So I turned to my best friend for help. But she just got me into trouble when she became fed up with me. She gave me a roof over my head to start with but in the end, when she'd had enough, she just got me arrested.

Why is it so difficult to talk to your family? Why do families react in such a way that their children feel they 'just couldn't grasp it'? They're often shocked and upset when they discover their child has a drug problem. One boy who was using speed regularly told us:

> My family were very distressed when they finally found out what had happened. They'd had their suspicions for a long time. I think their real problem was the guilt they went through. They kept asking themselves, where did we go wrong? They blamed themselves for what had become of me, despite the fact that I kept telling them I knew it was all of my own doing.

But when families recover from the shock, when they get

over the fear and distress, they can provide a lifeline. One young woman told us how she had gone to her parents and told them that she and her husband were heroin addicts. She told us:

> My parents were heartbroken. In fact my father was physically sick. But after they got over the shock they were wonderful. I don't know what we would have done without them. They made me and my husband realise what drugs were doing to us and how we would end up. Without them we would never have got off drugs.

Another woman explained how her family had first reacted when she told them she was addicted to LSD.

> My family felt both frightened for me and angry with me for having become an LSD addict. They all tried to help me get off. I was in a total mess at the time, especially mentally. But they stuck with me and arranged for me to get treatment.

One woman who is still battling to come off heroin told us:

> My husband is very good and understanding. He helps me to cut my intake down and he puts up with my moods and bad behaviour — behaviour which is often very nasty towards him. In helping me come off he's become more than just a husband; he's a friend and he's always there when I need him. And if I'm going to kick the habit, then I'm going to really need him.

Some families have gone for help themselves so they can try to understand the nature of the drug problem. One man who was a heroin addict told us:

> My mother and father went for counselling on how they could best help me. My mother was absolutely marvellous, encouraging and bolstering my morale. She was a major

factor in helping me to give up. When someone you really love is behind you it gives you that added reason and incentive to give up.

The encouragement which a family can offer when an addict is trying to give up seems to be very important. Perhaps this girl's words best sum up the importance of a supportive family.

... most of all they stood by me and cared and believed that one day I would stop – which I've now done.

Can professionals help?

We asked our drug users to tell us whether they had tried to find professional help to get them off their drugs. About half told us that they had sought professional help of various kinds. There were tremendous differences between the answers given according to what drug the user was taking regularly.

Of the heroin users, eighty-two per cent sought professional help; whereas only half the speed addicts and one in five of the cannabis plus users sought help. We then asked those who went for professional advice why they had done so. Most told us it was because they felt ill, or frightened. Family pressure was a significant reason, as was fear of arrest. Some users told us they had sought help because of the death of a friend through drugs and nearly as many because they felt there was 'more to life than drugs'. A few said they had gone for help because their job was threatened or they wanted to obtain a regular supply of drugs; some because they were unable to stop taking drugs and others because of their physical symptoms and debt. Two users mentioned suicide attempts as the reason for seeking professional help.

Can your GP help?

Nearly two thirds of those drug users who looked for professional help first turned to their GP. However sixty per cent of these people told us that they didn't find their GP helpful – it seems that the demands of a drug addict were more than most GPs could cope with. We were told how GPs 'just didn't want to know'. One man wrote:

I had to visit no less than six GPs before one would even listen to me. Most GPs don't want the bother of drug dependents on their books.

Another man who started smoking cannabis when he was eighteen and went on to become addicted to methadone and Diconal told us:

I went to my GP but he wasn't helpful. Most GPs don't want junkies on their books. I found that GPs are trained to know what's right. He didn't like being told what I thought I needed. But I think I knew more about drugs than he did.

The reference to general practioners not wanting 'junkies' was a common complaint.

I've had lots of GPs. It was my GP who was the first person I thought of when I wanted help but it wasn't useful. Some just gave me more drugs without question. Others just didn't want to know. In most cases the receptionist seemed to be told to say they're full if someone who seems to be a junkie walks into reception.

And even when a GP is willing to see someone with a drug problem, the lack of training in this field is a major obstacle.

My GP had no experience or knowledge of how to deal with a drug-related problem.

Or as one man who was a heroin addict told us:

When I realised I needed help I went to see my GP – he was the first person I thought of. My GP had always been a good doctor – compassionate, kind, the sort of doctor who always wanted to help with a problem. But over drugs he just had no idea how to help at all. I soon found out that most GPs have no idea how to help.

Unfortunately that man is still addicted to heroin and hasn't found a way of getting off drugs even though he wants to give up. Sadly some addicts are offered treatment which can compound the problem.

My GP just didn't know what to do. So he prescribed Valium for me. I thought it was just to get rid of me. He gave me the impression that he was relieved when I got out of the surgery.

Another doctor lectured the young man who'd sought his help:

The first time I went to see my GP for help, he just gave me a lecture. He told me that God didn't put me on earth to take drugs. I thought it was pretty naive advice so I just carried on taking drugs.

But some users admitted to seeking help from their doctors in order to ensure a steady supply of cheap or free drugs:

My GP used to give me heroin substitutes to try and get me off drugs. He thought he was just giving me a maintenance dose but I was using the service he offered for free drugs.

This of course explains why GPs are sometimes less than sympathetic in their attitude to drug addicts.

Users can also get help from private doctors working outside the NHS. Whilst most are very helpful, specialising in treating drug addicts, some are not. Their patients can actually get their drugs more cheaply than on the black market. One private patient told us:

Some private doctors know too little about drugs. When they do help they give out prescriptions far too easily and just profit on them.

So doctors are likely to react to drug users in one of three ways: they won't treat them, they can't treat them or they help. And when GPs are prepared to help, they can provide a most effective form of support.

One heroin addict told us:

> My GP was the first person I turned to when I decided to get help to come off drugs. He didn't know very much himself about the problem but he took the trouble to find out more about drugs and then arranged for me to get specialist help. He introduced me to a detoxification unit and I was gradually brought off drugs. I've been off heroin for over five months now. All thanks to the help of my GP.

Most people then, who look for help turn to their GP, but almost two thirds of users told us their doctors were not helpful. Either because they don't want to help or because they don't know how to help. If only GPs were able to act as the first port of call for all those needing help, they would provide that vital safety net filtering out the addicts they could treat effectively from those requiring more specialist treatment.

Hospital treatment

In the area of hospital treatment, services over the country are patchy. And the services themselves vary dramatically. Some hospitals have special facilities called DDUs or Drug Dependency Units where addicts undergo supervised withdrawal over weeks or sometimes even months. Invariably though, where they do exist, the waiting lists are long.

As one man who'd been a heroin addict since he was fourteen told us:

> I had to wait six months to get into a detoxification unit. It didn't work. It only dealt with the symptoms and not the problem. It was wholly ineffective. So far I've been in four detoxification units.

Another man who regularly takes a mixture of dope, heroin, DF118, solvents and various other drugs was not admitted to a specialist unit, but to a general psychiatric ward. He told us:

> I went to my GP first of all. He didn't know anything about drug abuse so he wasn't much help. He just said it was a phase I was going through. That was five years ago. Then I was sent to a hospital at last for 'specialist treatment'. I was admitted and put on a ward with mental patients. That was no help at all. After about four weeks I got drunk and was thrown out. I've had other stays in the same hospital since then. But the same thing happened. None of these places seem to understand the real problems of drug takers.

The survey offered plenty of criticism of hospital treatment. One woman who'd become addicted to Diconal, an opiate, told us:

> I was sent to a psychiatric ward when I went for treatment. I was treated as though I had lost my mind which didn't help at all. So I left after two days.

And another addict who used a whole range of drugs, from physeptone to amphetemines, from cannabis to Valium told us:

> First I went to see my doctor who prescribed barbiturates for me. I was just sixteen at the time and he gave me ever increasing doses to help counter the insomnia I suffered from speed. I ended up with an addiction to barbiturates. I voluntarily admitted myself to a psychiatric hospital to try and get help. There they told me 'No Drugs'. Consequently I got out as fast as I could. I wasn't ready to come off like that. I went back to the black market before I became too ill to move. It was an utter waste of time and the taxpayers money. I went back in again. Sometimes

they would try and coerce me with promises of drugs if I could hold on. They never came. They failed to grasp the simple fact that my fear of withdrawal symptoms was probably worse than coming off the drug itself.

One man who'd been addicted to heroin for many years explained why the hospital treatment he was given was so ineffective:

As soon as I'd arrived for any kind of treatment at the hospital I found I could just as easily leave and get a fix straight away. There was too much emphasis on group therapy sessions. The staff generally just didn't know how to deal with the needs of an addict, particularly emotional needs. (There didn't seem to be any genuine will to care). It became a challenge to try and cheat the consultants – that's probably why it didn't work the first time I was sent to a drug unit. It wasn't effective in the slightest because my personal problems – I was going through a divorce at the time – always came before my illness for me. Since then I've been in hospital so many times. When all is said and done, even the cleverest psychiatrist can only advise a junkie. It's getting the junkie to accept the advice that's the hardest part. In hospital they certainly never made me think twice.

It seems that the biggest criticism of hospital treatment is the lack of individual attention to the needs of a particular drug user who's trying to come off. One man who is still addicted to heroin and cocaine told us:

I had to wait nearly three months to get into a Drug Dependency Unit. I was given a prescription for oral methadone linctus on a withdrawal basis. This was ineffective because I wasn't given enough individual attention for my specific problems. The treatment they did give me just made me addicted to methadone instead of heroin. That's even harder to give up.

Rehabilitation

There are a growing number of residential rehabilitation centres in Britain. Some are long-term with treatment lasting several months – even years. Others are short-term, with courses lasting about six weeks. Most of the latter are private, rather than NHS establishments and can cost several hundred pounds per week. But if you do attend such a centre, it is likely you will have tried other methods of treatment and have failed at them. As one woman, a heroin addict explains:

> I first turned to my GP for help. She wanted to help but didn't know how. I think looking back I only wanted to con her for more drugs anyway. The people I spoke to didn't seem to have a clue. I was sent to a detoxification unit in a hospital but that didn't seem to work. I just went on taking drugs after I left. Then I was sent to a long-term residential centre, Alpha House. There I had to change my whole life-style. It did me a lot of good to learn and face up to the real world without the use of drugs.

Well, how do long-term residential centres work? Alpha House was the first of its kind in Europe. It is a very strict drug-free regime. Those who live there are offered a series of rewards and contracts for their success in avoiding drugs. Complete your contract and you move up in the hierarchy and gain privileges. Fail and you lose out.

Alpha House is basically about allowing people to have choices, different choices. The idea is to make the drug user see that they have limited themselves to choices about taking drugs and destroying their lives and their relationships. Alpha House expands the number of choices an individual can make, helps them see that they can be responsible for their own lives and the positive choices available to them.

There are encounter groups to get addicts to confront their problems and their failings. It's not easy. Addicts say it's very difficult especially at first. Many have come straight from prison and they should stay for about eighteen to twenty-four months.

Alpha House, which has been running for about seventeen years has kept detailed follow-up records of their ex-residents. They claim a success rate of just over fifty per cent for those who stay for four months and for those who stick out the full two-year course, nearly ninety-five per cent remain drug-free. Of course these figures don't include those who arrive at Alpha House and don't even manage to stay for four months. As one of those in our survey told us:

I was sent to a long-term rehabilitation centre after having been at a number of Drug Dependency Units for treatment, all of which had failed for me. However, the long-term centre was totally ineffective for me also. They tried to indoctrinate me and treated me as if I wasn't a free-thinking individual. They isolated me from the interests which would have helped me give up drugs – music, books. I needed these if I was ever going to get off drugs.

However most of those in our survey who had opted for long-term rehabilitation had positive things to say about centres like Alpha House. These were nearly always people who had been through a whole range of different treatments, like this woman, a heroin addict:

I first went to my GP. He was very good in some ways because his wife had been a junkie and he was very understanding. I was sent to a psychiatric unit and brought off the heroin I had become so addicted to. They used methadone and largactyl. It did stop me having bad withdrawal problems and physically I became free of drugs, but not mentally. I craved for them. I went back onto drugs after I left the hospital. I've had a lot of hospital treatment since but the same thing happens. It always works physically but not mentally – I always go back on it. Then I was sent to Alpha House where I learnt why I took drugs – the holes they were filling in my life. For me I believe this has been the answer to giving up. I'm now off altogether.

This lady has been receiving treatment at Alpha House for four months. She, together with many other addicts, endorses the view that the easy part of kicking a habit is overcoming the withdrawal symptoms – detoxification; the hard part is learning to live a drug-free life – rehabilitation.

Another heroin addict told us:

> My GP was terribly kind and patient but the treatment he gave me just didn't work. I wasn't entirely honest with him and I felt I was letting him down. In fact I think he should have guessed that I was cheating him. It had always been a problem for me to admit to myself that I was a junkie. The day finally came when I got caught forging a prescription for drugs and I was put on probation. That resulted in my being sent to hospital and being put on a psychiatric ward.
>
> I spent ten months in hospital – a long time by most people's experience of hospital care. They tried to get me off drugs by making me face up to reality. But I became institutionalised and indecisive as a result. I became a lap-dog. It was a terrible experience. When I came out I just started again. I was in and out of hospital four times.
>
> Then I heard about long-term rehabilitation where they teach you to reorganise your whole life and outlook. It's been extremely effective. I've been drug-free for over a year.

It would seem that success for people comes from the massive re-orientation they undergo in their whole outlook on life whilst living in these residential centres. As one man who'd become addicted to speed when he was seventeen told us:

> In hospital there just wasn't enough treatment to find out the reasons why you turn to drugs and end up leading such a destructive life. I had two lots of hospital treatment and it just didn't work. Then I managed to get eighteen months in a long-term centre. That has worked and I'm now drug-free. The reason it worked for me was because of the rehabilitation. Hospital treatment doesn't work because without rehabilitation it's so easy when you come out to go back on drugs again. You can't see why not to.

Rehabilitation treatment is based on changing the individual's outlook on life. One of the most well known of the short-term clinics is Broadway Lodge, based on an American idea know as the Minnesota Method. Addicts accept that they have an incurable disease. The only treatment possible is total abstinence from drugs. One man, addicted to cocaine, had received treatment at Broadway Lodge. He told us:

> The success for me by their method was coming to learn that I had a disease which is incurable but that I could recover from it. It would always be there waiting. But I can prevent it from happening.

There are a growing number of these clinics in Britain, and they claim a very high success rate. There is no doubt that some addicts find the idea of their addiction as an incurable illness very helpful in trying to kick the habit.

In the survey a number of people told us how they had come off drugs successfully by a variety of different methods – some self-imposed and others forced upon them. One man who'd been addicted to heroin from the age of seventeen told us:

> I first went to my GP. He called me a junkie and then kicked me out. He wasn't helpful at all.
>
> I managed to get specialist help at a hospital in London next. After six weeks I was thrown out. It was my own fault. I just couldn't get on with the kind of therapy classes they used.
>
> Then I was caught by the police for driving under the influence of drugs. A number of other convictions I'd got since taking drugs – burglary, shoplifting and possession – meant that I was given a prison sentence. I was sent to the Ley community prison. At first it was very, very hard. I had group therapy sessions twice a week which were very hard indeed. But through these I started to win back my own self-respect and trust. I spent eight months there but now I'm drug-free. I feel I owe my life to the staff who work

there. They made me realise that everything was my choice. I was the one who had to decide.

Other users also found that going to prison was the way they managed to get off drugs after the failure of any specialist long-term help they had previously received. One woman who'd been addicted to heroin since her late teens told us:

I'd been to see my GP who just said 'pull yourself together'. He wouldn't give me anything to help and offered no kind of treatment plan. He just kept saying it was a self-inflicted state. Then I got caught for burglary – I needed the money to pay for my heroin. I was sent to prison and there I couldn't get hold of any skag. It brought me to my senses and since then I've been drug-free.

But not everyone who spent time in prison was able to kick their habit. Of all the users in the survey over a quarter had been in jail since taking drugs. We asked them if they took drugs in prison and were surprised and rather alarmed when sixty-seven per cent said they did take drugs inside. For them, incarceration was clearly not the answer.

Because a lot of drug users are still at school when they really begin to have a problem, teachers are in a very important position to be able to help. One boy who'd started sniffing glue when he was ten and a half told us:

One day one of my teachers found me unconscious at school after a glue-sniffing session with my friends. The teacher was marvellous. He talked to me about what I was doing and how I could stop. He arranged for a counsellor to come and see me. The counsellor was marvellous. We talked about everything not just drugs and I came to trust her. I suppose it also helped because she wasn't old and she wasn't pushy. We built up a very good relationship just as if she was a school friend.

Others found help directly from their teachers. One girl told us about how she smoked cannabis regularly while she was at school and soon found that she couldn't cope without it. It was her teacher who managed to get her off when he found out:

My teacher was very patient and encouraging when he found out. He talked to me about what cannabis would do to my life. He explained what it might lead to and the crime that would come too. I'd end up with a criminal record he told me. He kept my confidence and I ended up stopping for him. His trust helped me a lot. I felt the teacher genuinely cared and I wanted to show him that I wouldn't become an addict and stopped altogether.

It seems that hand in hand with kicking drugs the user needs to believe in someone and feel that someone believes in them. It could be a teacher, a parent, a friend or as one girl told us it was her probation officer:

When I came out of prison my probation officer was marvellous. Two months after he finished seeing me officially I went back and asked if I could go on seeing him voluntarily. He said yes. He and I then worked out a programme to get me off speed. We made up a graph. I went to see him every week to report on how I was doing. I'd tell him whether I'd taken drugs or not and we'd mark it all on the graph. It helped enormously. Talking to someone who cares really matters. And he doesn't lecture me. I'm not off yet but if I do manage it it will be because of his encouragement.

Others turned to God and religion as a way of kicking the habit. One man who'd been addicted to tranquillisers told us:

My wife said that she was going to leave me. That made me realise I had to stop. I turned to Jesus Christ. I asked him to forgive me. I cried and cried for days after. I knew I was at the end of the road. It was this or nothing. Within

73

three days I found myself born again. I've never been so happy since that day and have been off ever since.

And a woman in our survey who'd also been addicted to tranquillisers told us:

My doctor told me I should go into a mental hospital. But my Minister of Religion said he would help me and become responsible for me. I was literally taken off the street and delivered from drugs through the name of Jesus Christ. Sixteen years later I'm still drug-free.

Giving up for good
Whatever method of treatment a drug addict may undergo, whoever he may find to help him, the one very clear message from our survey is that the drug user himself must want to stop taking drugs and, most importantly, want to stay off drugs thereafter. One young man who'd been addicted to heroin, methadone and Valium told us:

I was taken by my parents to see my GP, taken to hospital, sent to a psychiatric unit, given electric shock treatment, sent to a religious centre – the lot. Each time I managed to come off for a few months but then I went back on. I just wasn't ready to stop.

And another man who felt addicted to cannabis told us:

I didn't try and get specialist help because I knew that first I had to sort out what I wanted – the decision lay within myself whether or not I went on taking drugs.

As we were told repeatedly by addicts like this man:

Unless you really want to stop, any treatment is pointless. As most addicts know, stopping is pretty simple to manage. Staying off drugs after you've stopped is the real tester.

The majority of people in our survey who gave up successfully did so on their own, with neither help from their doctor nor a specialist treatment centre. They did it because they wanted to, not because someone else was trying to persuade them.

Often it seems addicts needed to change their lifestyle and in some cases their friends – the friends who might lead them back into taking drugs:

> I realised it wasn't a matter of staying off but changing my whole lifestyle, something I'm still doing.

> When you give up drugs you have to give up a way of life and sometimes completely change your friends.

And one drug addict told us about how he'd failed:

> I once managed to give up drugs for six months but the only people I know in life are users, dealers and drug-takers. So once I started mixing with them again I went back onto drugs.

Another man who'd been given hospital treatment told us why he had failed once he was discharged:

> Once I came out of hospital I found myself completely on my own. I had to cope with all the emotional problems I'd had before as well as trying to keep off drugs. With no help or back-up from anyone I started taking drugs again. I badly needed someone's support in those early days.

And another addict told us the same story:

> I'd been successfully weaned off drugs whilst I was in hospital. But as soon as I came out, back into reality, the real world again, I turned once more to drugs. I needed longer-term help. What was I going to do with all the time I suddenly found myself with, time when I used to take drugs? When you leave hospital you're on your own.

The route to coming off is hard. Addicts need someone to help them and believe in them and that help has to be long-term. They must develop a new way of life in which drugs cease to be the reason for existing. They have to find something else to fill the void created by removing their drug dependence.

Self-Help Groups

At the moment the voluntary sector is doing most for addicts and their families. They are distinct from the other services we've mentioned in this chapter because they are primarily *support* services for users and families; they don't provide treatment as such. The growing number of self-help groups, set up by families and users undertake a lot of advice work. But they are poorly financed and resourced and, not suprisingly, their services are patchy.

Narcotics Anonymous and Families Anonymous (with groups around the country) are vital in the network of help and advice services but they and are unable to offer a nationwide service.

In addition there are numerous other self-help groups, funded in a variety of ways, all over the country – though not coordinated nationally. Some have grown up from parental concern and exist to help the families of drug users; others offer counselling and advice and some act as pressure groups, lobbying for better facilities and services for addicts.

On *Drugwatch* we ran a phone-in to try to extend the existing register of self-help groups and to put people in touch with others who were interested in setting up new groups. One hundred groups were placed on a central register as a result of our phone-in, many of them coming to the attention of the authorities for the first time. This updated register of groups is being made available to doctors, counsellors, libraries and Citizens Advice Bureaux as part of the 'National Directory of Services for Drug Users' which was published as a result of the *Drugwatch* programme.

The Way Ahead

Clearly, we need a wide-ranging and varied collection of methods for helping drug addicts come off drugs. Different things work for different people.

Government funding has increased, but our evidence shows that it's still not enough. If a drug addict feels he needs help, then the help must come quickly. Waiting lists are a huge obstacle to effective treatment. The response must be instant. Nearly fifty per cent of those who wanted treatment had to wait more than two months:

One month	31%
Two months	21%
Three months	14%
Four months	4%
Five months	2%
Six months	14%
Over six months	12%

Table 15: Waiting time for specialist treatment

It is clear that long waiting periods are no help to drug users. One of the major obstacles to a drug addict getting off drugs is recognising, like alcoholics, that they have a problem in the first place. Once they take that very difficult step and confront their problem, they need help straightaway. It seems appalling that just under half of those who wanted specialist treatment should have to wait more than two months before they could get the help they needed.

One very strong message emerging from the survey was that people turn first to their GPs when they want help. We know that many found their GPs unhelpful and that some were even turned away. However there is still a positive sign here. When trying to get help for a problem you need to know where to go. It seems that drug addicts turn to their GP as a matter of course. So what we clearly need to do is help doctors understand the problems of addicts and equip them to cope with the scale and complexities of the problem. GPs need to be trained in the management of patients with drug problems. They need to understand the demands of a drug addict. Most of all they need to know when and how to refer patients they can't help for specialist treatment.

Drug abuse is not a passing phenomenon. It is a problem that will not simply go away. It needs to be brought into the mainstream services that doctors and social services currently provide.

The fact is that treatment and help for addicts seems to lag a long way behind the problem. Over and again users say they need a comprehensive, quick-responding service if they are successfully going to kick the habit.

4. THE END OF THE LINE

Deaths from drug addiction are rare. Few people die from the drugs themselves; but the substances with which drugs are sometimes mixed can prove fatal. And what is more, if a user normally takes a very impure form of the drug, a pure dose can prove fatal. But drug users are more likely to have accidents which can be life-threatening.

Some surveys completed by families told us about users who had died as a result of taking drugs. What was frightening about these surveys was the striking similarities between their lives and those of users who were still alive. The addict who dies shares the same profile as the addict who survives. In many cases death resulted from a tragic accident.

In this chapter we have taken the stories of several of those families and retold them, some briefly and one at length. They are drug users who have died of overdoses; of drugs mixed with poisonous material; and of accidents which happened while they were stoned or tripping.

Peter's story

We heard about Peter from his mother. Peter started taking drugs when he was just thirteen. Three years later he died; he'd become addicted to solvents:

> Peter started sniffing glue while he was at school. He did it because all his friends were doing it and they told him of all the beautiful dreams they had when they sniffed glue. He didn't want to be called a chicken so he tried it.
>
> He became addicted to glue sniffing. He used to buy it in the local shops – Evo-stick, glue pens and paint strippers. When I found out I was horrified. I used to sit and talk to

Peter for hours about the damage to his health. But I didn't know how I could help.

I went to our social worker first of all. I went to my doctor next. He knew of the problem and he suggested I go to my Citizens Advice Bureau to see if they could help me find a drug group. So I went to them but they said there wasn't one.

I tried everywhere for help. I even tried the police but all I was ever told was that it was a phase and Peter would grow out of it. I now think that the authorities just didn't know how to cope with the problem.

Peter didn't grow out of his phase as they called it. He went on with his glue sniffing. When he was fifteen he tried to commit suicide. He slashed his wrists after a glue sniffing session. Fortunately he failed. But then three weeks later after another glue sniffing session he took his own life by hanging himself. We'll never know whether he was very high on glue at the time or not or whether he was just very depressed.

Caroline's Story

Caroline's mother wrote to tell us about her daughter who died four years ago. Caroline had been introduced to drugs by her boyfriend Simon. She told us:

My daughter was sixteen when she met her boyfriend. He was on drugs at the time. He gave her her first injection of heroin. He kept her supplied and got her addicted.

When I realised what was happening I tried to get them apart. They had a love-hate relationship. For us it was all full of trauma and unhappiness. We watched Caroline, completely unable to cope with this relationship, getting worse and worse. We watched the effects that drugs had on her – she seemed to use them to lessen the misery of her relationship much of the time. Her boyfriend used to beat her up sometimes and she would take drugs to ease the pain she went through. She wouldn't leave him though.

Eventually her boyfriend died. That tore her apart. I tried to get help, but there was nowhere to go. Very few people seemed to know anything about drugs. I saw various doctors and tried to convince them that my daughter was an addict. They said she's experimenting, it's a phase – that kind of thing. One even told me I was paranoid. It was like banging my head against a brick wall. No one listened.

Some suggested that I should throw my daughter out if I really wanted to help. That I should forget her because if she was addicted she was rotten. I couldn't have lived with myself if I'd done that to my daughter. It might have been easier just to throw her out and forget her in some ways but I loved her very much and I just couldn't do it, whatever the price to my own life. I was full of pity for her. We tried to make her life as comfortable as we could and we know she appreciated what we did.

Over the next few years we noticed her health collapse. She lost the proper use of her arms because of injecting. All her veins collapsed, her teeth rotted and she became painfully thin. She was awfully unhappy and depressed. Her sight started to fail and she complained often of blurred vision. Gradually she began to lose her will to live.

My daughter wasn't living with us at the time she died. But I used to go and see her often. One day I went over to her flat. I found her in bed. I knew that she was dying. I felt that Caroline knew that her life was over too. I looked at what was left of our once beautiful daughter and said goodbye to her and walked away.

I went home and told my husband. We didn't tell anyone else because we knew they didn't care about her. My husband went over to her flat straightaway. She was already dead.

In life Caroline looked like an old woman, full of pain and misery. In death her face was free of pain and she looked young again. Her torment was over.

Her death certificate read, 'Cause of Death: Chronic Drug Addiction'. Her death brought an end to her tormented existence. She'd had every drug-related illness you could name. Her body was scarred all over from the injections. She had lived in hell.

Richard's story

Richard began taking speed when he was in his teens. His father thought he was probably less than fourteen the first time he tried it.

I realised that he'd started because of his friends, not pushers – that was a surprise to me. His friends were all children of well-off families. They introduced him to drugs and all-night discos where they took them. Richard came from a good, stable working-class home. One of his friend's was a doctor's son. He used to steal prescription pads from his father and use them to get drugs.

Richard soon became addicted. But he didn't want to be. He wanted to come off. We went to see our GP. We asked for help, but he didn't seem to care.

Even though he was addicted Richard got married and had children. Again and again he tried to come off. Once he managed to get treatment in a hospital. It was useless though because they allowed all his junkie friends to come and visit him. They just brought him drugs.

The only time he ever really came off drugs was when he was sent to prison. He'd been convicted of burglary – a crime he committed because he needed the money for his drugs. Away from his wife and friends he was able to stay virtually drug-free. He told me that occasionally he got drugs in prison but this was mostly cannabis. Heroin and cocaine are harder to get in prison.(I know all this to be true because I'm a prison officer; drugs do get into prison and prisoners do take them.)

As soon as he came out of prison he became addicted again. I think it happened because his wife is an addict and the only people he seemed to know were drug addicts. They were always in his house. He couldn't get away from the drug scene.

My son died just a few months ago after a massive drug overdose. He'd been given a huge injection of diamorphine: he hadn't given it to himself because he couldn't. He'd wrecked nearly all the veins in his body except one because of injecting into them all the time.

My son has died as a result of taking drugs. I have one other son and I'm afraid because I know that Richard has introduced him to drugs and I think he now may be an addict. But there doesn't seem to be anything I can do.

Sally's story

We heard about Sally from her sister Louise. Sally started taking drugs when she was fourteen. Her sister found out a year later. She was taking barbiturates – the drug Tuinal.

I first noticed something was wrong when Sally started to behave irrationally about all kinds of things. I couldn't speak to her anymore without her behaving very oddly. Then I noticed that some of my clothes started to go missing. When I asked her if she knew what had happened to them she said that she'd sold them to friends. I found out that she'd started because of her friends. I think she took drugs as a way out of problems too. My parents often used to quarrel and I think it upset her a lot.

Sally then started shoplifting to pay for new drugs. She used to steal clothes and then sell them to get quick cash to buy her Tuinal.

To get help I went with her to see a social worker and, when that didn't work, our doctor. He referred us to various Child Guidance Clinics. He was very helpful. He tried everything he knew – he even tried hypnosis. But Sally couldn't give up drugs. We found again and again that most professional people just don't know anything about drugs.

My sister then moved out into a squat. One day she took eighteen Tuinal and a hundred Panadol. She wasn't found for three days. She was still alive and was taken to hospital. For seven days she was kept alive. But she died. Her liver had completely failed and with it every organ in her body packed up. She was eighteen years old.

Garry's story.

We heard about Garry from his mother. It is a poignant story, told by a very loving and caring parent:

My son Garry was born at 5.50 p.m. on 11th January, 1966 in the British Military hospital in Isserlohn, West Germany. He was a much wanted son, as I had suffered five miscarriages after the birth of his sister Elaine. From the minute he was born he was a special little boy, so full of loving, never any trouble, always content and happy.

Twenty-two months after his birth Garry got a little brother Stephen, but this only seemed to make him happier and as children the three of them were always very close. In February 1969 Garry's father and I separated – his father staying in England and myself and the three children returning to Ayr in Scotland to live with my widowed father. Garry and his natural father were never very close. This was due to the fact that Garry was a quiet-natured wee boy and his father used to try and bully him into being a tougher person, but it wasn't in Garry to be boisterous or tough. He liked nothing better than to come up on my knee for a kiss and cuddle, then he would stroke my cheek look up at me his eyes full of love and say, 'My Mum, My Mum. I never, throughout his life as a baby, young child or teenager ever needed to scold Garry or reprimand him.

He and his grandfather were the best of pals, every hour he was not at school he spent sitting at home with his grandfather or, his 'Papa' as Garry called him. In the meantime I had remarried and my children all loved my new husband. They never at any time regarded him as a step-father.

Garry especially loved him; he had found in my husband William a kind, loving and very understanding Dad – one who knew Garry was special. Many hours they spent in each other's company, either fixing the car or doing some work in the garden.

When he was about fourteen years old Garry was having a lot of difficult times at school. We thought he was not very academic but the truth was that his reserved nature was causing him problems. He preferred not to do some of his lessons in case he got them wrong, thus getting into trouble. His teacher at school, instead of understanding Garry's problems, actually harrassed him. This, in turn, caused Garry to start playing truant from school. It was whilst being truant Garry started hanging about an amusement arcade newly opened in the town. This was a good hiding place, out of the public eye. He met and took up company with a young man called Jonny who was a twenty-one year old veteran of trouble, remand homes, detention centres, police, and courts, who came from a broken home. He was also a drug user and pusher. This part I only found out when Garry's drug problem came out.

It was only a matter of time before Jonny introduced Garry to the life of stealing. They broke into a shop, got caught and were up in court the next morning. Jonny got three months in jail. Garry got two years in a reform school which was nearly two hundred miles away from Ayr. I thought that day my world had collapsed and wondered how my lovely, innocent boy of just fifteen years was going to survive in a place like that. I cried night and day worrying about him. However, it was the best thing that could have happened to Garry. The headmaster and teachers at Rossi Farm School took Garry to their hearts and right away we were invited up to see the school and meet them. This I did with much apprehension. I will never forget the feelings I had when I stood back and looked up at that big house for the first time. Inside however, was a different story. Garry greeted us with his usual lovely smile, a kiss for me right away, then we were served tea. Immediately I asked Garry – 'Oh son, what kind of place is this?' Garry answered me with this statement, 'They're strict Mum, but fair.' I suddenly realised my boy had grown up.

I think the ten months Garry spent in Rossi Farm must have been quite happy ones. His schooling immediately improved. His teacher there knew just how to bring out the best in him, and his attitude towards sports changed. He won two major sports awards; one for gymnastics; one for canoeing. He went rock climbing, skiing, camping. He also learned several trades. Thanks to the headmaster and teachers Garry was released after only ten months. The head teacher said he should never have been sent there in the first place.

Rossi Farm School got Garry a summer job at one of the hotels near Montrose. He actually went first as a gardener/handyman, but when the hotel owner saw him he said, 'You're too handsome a young man to be a handyman. You'll look good in my dining room' and he put Garry in charge of six young student waitresses. This act was to bring out something more in Garry; he discovered he could be quite a hit with the ladies.

When his summer job finished he returned to Ayr and got a job with the Youth Opportunities Programme as a bricklayer. Garry was by now a very handsome young man. He had four friends who too were very handsome and for about a year the five of them had about every girl in Ayr running after them. For them the world was their oyster. They were five very popular, happy young men. Unknown to us Jonny had returned to the town from one of his jail sentences and had met Garry again. Somewhere along the line he had introduced Garry to smoking cannabis.

The first time I saw Garry with a cigarette I couldn't believe it, for as a child he hated smoking and couldn't stand the smell. I didn't make a big thing about his smoking as the rest of the boys seemed to be doing it. Then one day I went into Garry's room for something. There was a strong sweet smell. I mentioned it to my daughter Elaine who quite innocently informed me it was cannabis. I nearly collapsed at what Elaine was telling me. She in turn could not understand why I was getting so worked up as it was the 'done thing' – a phase that Elaine assured me would pass. After all, she too had smoked cannabis but gave it up as it did nothing for her and was too expensive. But alas this phase was not to pass for Garry. No indeed, it was just the beginning of the end for my kind, loving, innocent son. Garry was just sixteen years old and was now on the road to destruction and death. I tried several times to get my once-so-close son to talk to me about his cannabis smoking but Garry would not have it. In fact he completely denied even taking the stuff. Eventually I stopped even thinking about it, after all, Garry seemed to be alright. In fact he never looked better. He had developed a more outgoing nature; had gained confidence in himself, did not appear to be getting into any trouble with the police or anything, so maybe I was making a big thing out of nothing. God knows I have lived to regret those thoughts.

Life for us went on as usual but then on the 9th September 1982 my father died. He had an illnes of only five weeks – cancer of the bowel. Garry never really accepted his Papa's death. He never came to terms with it. It was obvious he was greatly affected by it all. Nine months later we moved house, and as none of us were happy living there after my father's death, I thought the move was best for all of us. Just after we moved I met Jonny in the town one day and during our conversation he informed me that I would need to do something about Garry and his involvement with drugs. He told me that Garry was now a dealer. He was the dealer for our housing scheme. I was absolutely devastated by Jonny's story. Firstly, I consulted Garry, but of course all was denied. Jonny had given me names, addresses, days and times, so after much thought and deliberation I knew there was only one thing I could do – go to the police and tell all.

As I knew the Chief of Ayr police personally I went to him and told him about Garry's own drug habit and how he was a dealer. The police chief told me I had done the right thing coming to him and that he would send a C.I.D. officer out to see me at home. I left that man that day with a very heavy heart but I just knew I had to do it if I was to get my boy out of this thing he was so deeply involved in. Well to this day no police came to see me at home. Nothing was ever done about Garry's trafficking. On several occasions I approached the police. I told them about people, places in the town where the drug dealing was going on but to my horror the police said they were not interested. They knew all about the people and places but these were just small fish. They were waiting for the big fish.

By now the change in Garry was drastic. He had split up with his four friends and his new acquaintances were all weird looking characters. Garry himself was not working. He had stopped taking an interest in his once immaculate appearance, stayed out all night most nights and when at home did not mix with the rest of the family. He spent all his time locked in his room. The only times he came into the living room was to take the continuous phone calls he was getting. People called at the door but they were always quickly usheredup stairs to his room. I confronted them on several occasions telling them that I knew exactly what they were there for. I threatened to tell their parents and to report Garry and them to the police, but they didn't bother with my threats.

During February Garry was out of the house after one of our now frequent rows. He was sleeping rough here, there and anywhere. I never locked the doors when Garry was out of the house. It was always open in case he came home. Garry returned home the first week in March. It was terrible – arguments all the time. Garry was now very aggressive towards his sister and brother, hitting out at them. He even hit me a couple of times. In fact he had nothing but contempt for his sister and me. But he also had outbursts of crying and he appeared to be going out of his mind sometimes. I phoned the doctor on three occasions but he always refused to come out because it was not Garry who was asking for him to come. In desperation I searched for someone to help me save my son. Eventually my daughter and I found a drug rehabilitation centre in a town about sixteen miles from Ayr. At the centre all we got was some counselling on how we should behave towards Garry and his drug-taking. When Garry found out about us visiting the centre he went berserk and accused me of trying to get him put away. On Thursday 21st March Garry had one of his phone calls and during the conversation the words, 'half a gram', were mentioned. 'Yes, I can handle that', said Garry. After he left the room Elaine said to me, 'Did you hear that conversation Mum?', when I said I had, she said, 'Well there is only one drug you get in half grams – heroin Mum'.

Throughout the last year I had been keeping watch on Garry's arms for needle marks, but Garry was one step ahead of me. He had in fact been using his thighs or torso, knowing full well that there was little chance of my ever seeing those parts of his body. On Friday 22nd March a boy called at the house to see Garry. Elaine went up to tell him. She walked into his room to find Garry trying to hide a syringe and needle and his girlfriend was trying to hide a packet of white powder. Garry immediately denied the syringe was his, saying he was holding it for someone. Elaine didn't answer him but when she came back into the living room she told her Dad and me what she had just seen. We decided there and then to phone the police and tell them that we thought our son had heroin in the house. The police were there in about five minutes and as they were taking Garry away he turned to me and said in a quiet voice, 'Mum, you grassed me'. I answered him by saying, 'I certainly have son'. Garry was brought back home after about an hour. He had been charged with being in possession with intent to supply. The incident was not discussed again; in my mind I had stopped my son from taking his first fix of heroin. We were later to discover Garry had in fact been on heroin for six months.

From the Sunday onwards, Garry became quite nauseated. Sometimes a bit argumentative. He became quite lethargic and sleepy, very withdrawn. I explained to the rest of the family that this was the start of withdrawal signs, as we believed that Garry had not had any drugs for a few days. But tragically unknown to us his girlfriend had taken Garry into the town on the Saturday morning and paid for a 'fix' for him from another dealer. A young girl I may add. The 'fix' she gave Garry was doctored with ninety per cent paracetamol mixture. For the rest of the week Garry continued to sleep a lot, shout a bit when awake and vomit from time to time. I came in at 7.30 a.m. on Friday 29th March to hear Garry vomiting in his room. I decided that I would phone for the doctor. Maybe Garry would need medical help to get him through the withdrawal period. As I started up the stair, there was Garry standing at the top, death was on his face. I rushed up to him and for the first time in months I saw him without the big old black coat he was always wearing. Suddenly I realised the weight loss my son had suffered. I put my arms round him and I said, 'Garry you are going to have to let me get the doctor out to you son'. He looked at me, his eyes so sad and lifeless and he said to me, 'Yes Mum, 'cause I am no' well, I'm no' well.' I helped him down to the toilet as he felt sick. As I got him into the toilet he started to vomit fresh blood. It was just pouring from his mouth. He collapsed on the toilet floor. I screamed for my daughter and between us got him back upstairs to his bed. I phoned for the doctor at 8.10 a.m. but it was 12.20 p.m. before he came. At first he was quite cheeky with us, asking Garry what drug he had been taking. The doctor was standing so far back from Garry's bedside he hadn't notice that Garry was comotose. When I turned Garry's face round to him the doctor said, 'God, we will need to get this boy to hospital.'

Garry was admitted to a medical unit but later on that day he was transferred to another hospital, an infectious disease unit as they now thought Garry had hepatitis. I left Garry in hospital that night thinking that at last he had a chance of breaking his drug habit. The first thing next morning the hospital phoned for me to come up right away as they were having some trouble with Garry. On arriving at the hospital the doctors told me that they had tried to have Garry transferred to a psychiatric hospital during the night as he had become a bit violent and uncooperative with the staff. The truth of the matter was that my once lovely boy was dying and nobody realised it, least of all me. They took me in to see him. The scene that met me that morning will stay in my mind forever. The room was like a battle field, drip stands lying on the floor, furniture overturned and Garry was lying on the bed with nothing on but a pyjama jacket. His arms and legs were covered in bruising and bite marks. Five people were holding him down. His eyes were staring out of his head and he was frothing from the mouth. He was screaming, 'I want my Mam, I want my Mam.' The Sister told me he had been screaming that all morning. I took his head in my arms and started to tell him it was alright, his Mam was here. But Garry just stared into my face and then tried to bite me. He was like a mad dog, biting himself, banging his head on the wall. I became hysterical so they took me out of the room. I stayed at the hospital until 4.20 a.m. on the Sunday morning and when I left Garry was sleeping quietly on a mattress on the floor of his room. I knew my son's medical condition was serious but I thought it was due to the hepatitis and although I knew he was very ill I was glad he would be spared the horror of going through the withdrawal from his drugs. For with him being so ill due to the hepatitis, by the time he got over that he would be free from the drug need as well. I returned home about 5.00 a.m. I phoned the hospital on the hour for the next three hours and each time I was told there was no change in Garry.

At 8.20 a.m. on Sunday 31st March I had a phone call from the doctor at the hospital telling me to get to the Southern General Hospital in Glasgow as soon as possible as Garry was being transferred to the neurosurgical unit there. I got to the hospital at 9.25 a.m. and at 10.15 a.m. the consultant told me that my son was going to die. There was nothing the medical profession could do to save the life of my once eleven and a half stone, handsome boy who was now down to seven and a half stone. Suddenly from somewhere I drew strength. I sent my family home. They were absolutely shattered and I did not want them to have to watch their brother suffer anymore. On Tuesday Garry was put on a life-support machine and when I was taken into see him, a young life wasted through drugs, I knew then he was not going to die in vain. Somehow I had to let all the young people know how a drug addict spends his last days. I contacted a national newspaper and invited them to the hospital to see my son. But the doctors would not allow this, so I got my husband to take a photo of Garry on his death bed connected to all the machinery that was keeping him alive. The paper of course published Garry's story, showed that horrific picture and claimed it shocked the nation – but did it? How many young people were really affected by the picture? How many parents took heed from my story? I can answer both these questions on behalf of my own town of Ayr; very, very few – if any.

Garry died at 3.30 a.m. on the 6th April, 1984, age eighteen years. I have asked myself a million times, how did it all happen? Why did it happen to my precious, lovely wee boy? And the only answer I can come up with is, if it takes one drug addict to die so that more addicts and would-be addicts can be saved and my Garry had to be that one, so be it then.

We will never forget Garry. The lovely baby, the happy content wee boy, and the so shortened life of the kind considerate young man.

Garry the drug addict, who was he?

5. PREVENTION

We asked people in our survey to give us their suggestions for the most effective way to prevent young people from taking drugs. One mother wrote:

> Much stiffer sentences for drug pushers when they're caught and more effort by the police to catch the street pushers.

One problem with this suggestion is that it's the users' friends not just pushers and dealers you have to beware of. Forty-nine per cent of the heroin users were found to be selling heroin regularly to their friends; fifty-seven per cent of speed users were pushing to their friends and sixty per cent of cannabis users were introducing their friends to drugs. Policing this network would be impossible.

What about the importers and the drug barons? From our users' survey came the view that the police and customs should do more to catch the people who are making large amounts of money out of drugs; coupled with that they believed the police should ease off the addict and occasional drug-user:

> It is about time the law was changed and the police concentrated their efforts on the importers of heroin instead of coming down on people for smoking dope. Dope has the same effect as alcohol. In which case why aren't the police arresting alcoholics addicted to alcohol?
> I feel that it is very important that the police concentrate

their efforts on following a source through until they find the financiers behind the drugs importation rather than continually harrassing known users. Often sending users to prison only teaches them to become criminals – it doesn't usually give them the medical help they need to come off.

Can we halt the drugs problem at source, destroy the crops and the illegal laboratories? The short answer is no. Drug trafficking is an international business and controlling it is an international problem. And efforts in this field so far have yielded minimal returns. For example, since 1972 the United States has financed schemes in Thailand to encourage producers to grow vegetable crops rather than drug crops. But these efforts have been unsuccessful – the old crops grow alongside the new.

Most of the West's heroin comes from the 'Golden Crescent', the border areas of Pakistan and Afghanistan. Despite huge efforts, heroin continues to be exported on a vast commercial scale. In South America it is thought that production of cocaine has tripled in the last seven years despite international efforts to control trafficking. One laboratory found in the heart of the Amazon had been used for refining cocaine and produced enough to supply the annual United States demand four times over.

The best the West can do is disrupt production. It can't control it or stop it altogether. Last year the United States spent over a billion and a half dollars in their fight against drugs and did little to effect the volume of trade.

Can we stop the drugs from getting into this country? Can customs do more? The short answer again is no. The smugglers are clever. Their contraband is very portable and easy to conceal and the rewards for the risks they are taking are enormous. Customs officers are understaffed and under-resourced. It is totally impractical to try and control drugs by searching everything and everyone coming through an airport or port. In creating 'Fortress Britain' you would bring the country to a standstill.

What about the police in Britain – can they do more to try

and catch those who distribute drugs on a large scale to the pushers and dealers? There is no doubt they have some success. But it's a slow and costly business to achieve even limited success.

We examined a police operation in *Drugwatch*. The Sussex Police and Customs in 1980 concluded a very successful swoop which resulted in over a ton and a half of cannabis being seized. But that operation – 'Yashmak' – led the police into another bigger and much more sophisticated drugs ring.

During the investigation Paul Joseph Parker was seen visiting drug dealers but detectives had no evidence against him. Once 'Yasmak' was over Parker became the focus of the police's attention. 'Operation Bentley' had now begun.

Police watched Parker at his home on the Sussex coast. They established where he went and who he saw. Cars parked outside the house were watched and followed. The police set up an incident room to monitor information. They were soon able to monitor the deals made in pubs and hotels. Money in one pub, drugs in another and Joe Parker in a third.

After several months the police established the identity of the dealer Gerald Karakanna, and the storeman and cutter, Colin Brown. Parker was the brains and the money behind the ring. But at this stage detectives still did not know which drug was being traded. To find that out they decided to stop Karakanna under cover of a routine traffic offence. In the car they found bags of cocaine worth over twelve thousand pounds.

More officers were brought in. Three months later they were ready for the kill. In a pub in Kent Parker made a huge blunder. He needed cocaine for his own use and he met the third man Colin Brown to get his supplies. Parker had finally broken his own rule because he was now carrying the drugs himself. The detectives seized their chance and moved in and arrested both Parker and Brown.

They then moved quickly and that night sixty people were arrested. A quarter of a million pounds was seized as well as rifles, pistols, ammunition and drugs.

Parker made statements that ran to more than a hundred and sixty pages and provided the police with vital leads to the key figures on the international scene.

One of these men was Ahmed Andalusi – a cocaine importer. Born in Morocco, based in Brazil, he'd slipped through the police net twice before detectives finally caught up with him in London. From Andalusi, Sussex detectives traced a drug trail through Switzerland where the money was kept, and Portugal where his couriers stayed and finally back to his luxury home in Brazil.

In all, twenty-five people received sentences totalling more than a hundred and twenty years. Andalusi received twelve. Parker was given six. A classic police operation. It took two years and thousands of hours of police time.

How successful was 'Operation Bentley?' Detective Chief Inspector John Rees who led the police operation, told us:

There is little doubt that the arrests made under Operation Bentley caused the price of cocaine in this country to rise considerably. But this only lasted three to four weeks because I'm sure there were some other persons who were soon to jump in and fill the vacuum caused by the arrests.

Successful – yes, but also disappointing. Is there more the police could do? We asked Detective Chief Superintendent Roy Penrose, Head of the Central Drug Intelligence Squad. He felt the police could do more provided they were given more resources. But he believes within the problem of drug abuse, law enforcement is just one aspect. He regards law enforcement as the centre of an operation which is linked to education and prevention to stop people swelling demand, and to treatment and rehabilitation to curtail demand by those already addicted.

One new initiative is likely to be effective. It has already proved so in the United States. New legislation will allow the Courts to seize assets from convicted drug traders. The deterrent effect is important, provided of course the profits have not been laundered so effectively that the police are unable to lay claim to them.

However, whatever steps the police and government's take it's the people who take drugs who will ultimately determine whether the drug trafficker is beaten. You can make it a risky business to supply drugs but you can't actually halt the supply unless the demand itself dries up.

We have learnt from the survey that most people when they start taking drugs are still living at home. In fact, since they first take drugs in their own homes or those of friends, perhaps parents could do much more to combat the problem. But what can they do? What should they do?

In the United States there are two national parents' associations which were formed to fight drug abuse among young people. 'Pride' and 'Parents for a Drug-Free Youth' have a huge following across the country. We looked at a group of such parents in Florida. They don't just restrict their campaign to illegal drugs but include tobacco and alcohol too. They set up a stall in a major shopping mall every Saturday and provide free leaflets and information sheets on drugs. Other volunteers have formed Parent Peer Groups – an opportunity for parents to get together and talk about drug-related problem, their anxieties and experiences. They discuss how to keep their children away from drugs, how to warn parents of the dangers and how to make sure that their children are kept away from the temptation as they get older.

Parents have to agree on the principle of no drug use whatsoever. They think an adult should be in the background of all children's activities, no matter how old the children are – teenagers as well as tots. For example, they held a drug and alcohol-free graduation party attended by chaperones! They also 'Courtwatch' – they observe court proceedings and make sure that the media are informed of leniency shown by judges in sentencing convicted drug pushers. It all seems rather extreme, a somewhat 'un-British' way of reacting.

Could organisations like these work in Britain? We asked drug users in our survey to tell us about the role they think parents can and should take to control drug abuse. The notion of stricter parental control came bottom of their list.

When we asked drug-users to tell us what they thought

would be most helpful in preventing people from trying drugs, they gave us this list of suggestions in order of priority.

1. More education about drugs in schools.
2. More publicity about the dangers of drug use.
3. Better job prospects for young people.
4. Better communication between parents and children.
5. Fewer TV programmes and articles which glamourise drug use.
6. Tougher police action against suppliers of drugs.
7. Less liberal attitude by parents to drug-use.

Users placed the need for education at the top of the list. More than seventy per cent of our users thought it was vital. Given the age at which so many people start it seems very good advice. Just what kind of education however was the subject of divergent opinion in our survey. One group felt that shocking young people was the answer:

I believe that children should be shown the horrors of drug abuse, at school when they're say eleven years old. It should be shown without censorship and aimed at shocking them. To many children today, drugs are a household word, as harmless as coffee and cornflakes.

Others felt that shock tactics were self-defeating:

When I was at school they just used to tell us to stay away from drugs because they can hurt you. That just made me inquisitive about drugs and more willing to try them. But I do think education is the answer but it must be a proper course of organised education which really explores the subject and looks truthfully at the effects of taking drugs.

What is being done in our schools at the moment? Not a great deal. Seventy per cent of our schools have no formal teaching about drugs. One organisation, TACADE, the Teachers Advisory Council on Alcohol and Drug Education currently produces special information packs and trains teachers to organise classes about drugs. Children need to learn how to resist the pressure of being called 'chicken' by their friends if they don't want to take the drugs. They need to learn how to say no.

In fact *learning to say no* may well be part of the answer. We all know that it is easier to say yes than to say no. And teaching children how to say no is difficult. It cannot be done effectively in one lesson, by a visiting expert. It must be part of a well-intergrated curriculum. An effective American campaign designed to keep children from smoking cigarettes was part of the daily school curriculum, part of normal lessons. It was taught by teachers who had been specially trained but who also knew the children they were teaching. The key element was to teach the youngsters to stand on their own two feet. So that when the moment came when they were offered cigarettes they could refuse with confidence.

The campaign was carefully evaluated and was found to have worked. Children smoked less and when they did smoke, they started later.

In this country a campaign like that could work too. One of the biggest problems teachers face is their own ignorance about the subject. They are not trained to teach this kind of health education course and share many commonly held misconceptions about drugs.

The only way to fight the drugs problem is to attack it on all fronts: at school, in the family, through the media, using community organisations, by informed opinion and with the help of trained doctors, nurses, police, social workers and teachers and above all by informed young people – those who will have to make the choice.

This means reaching children when they're very young. As the survey shows the average age at which people are likely to start is when they are still young teenagers. We need to educate our children about drug abuse when they are eleven or twelve. Those lessons need to be reinforced and developed as the child gets older.

Schools can help directly. Special drug education classes incorporated regularly into the curriculum would be effective in preventing young people from taking drugs.

99

6. ADVICE FROM DRUG USERS

Towards the end of the survey we asked people to consider a series of propositions about drug-taking. Nearly all the users, whatever drugs they took, agreed that not enough was being done at present to help people with drug problems.

Interestingly, when we asked whether most drug-takers actually need help, five times more regular heroin users answered 'yes' than those people using cannabis, which illustrates rather neatly how different drugs effect users lives in dramatically different ways. This is often overlooked by those issuing a blanket condemnation of *all* drugs.

It is worth noting that the effect of such a blanket condemnation can result in experimentation with more serious drugs. Young people with a little experience of say, cannabis, know that it doesn't kill or inevitably lead to the user becoming a 'junkie'. So when they are advised to steer clear of all drugs, because they're deadly, they can be expected to disregard the warning as fraudulent. If the warning is factually incorrect about the effects of smoking cannabis, they say it is likely to be wrong about heroin. So shock tactics are likely to be at best ineffective and at worst counter productive, resulting in increased curiosity to experiment.

We listed eleven measures which have been suggested as ways to help users. We asked users to list these ideas in order of priority:

1. More training for GPs in how to help drug users
2. More treatment facilities within the NHS
3. More information and advisory services for the families of drug users

100

4. More long term rehabilitation centres
5. More sympathetic response from GPs
6. Better employment prospects for ex-users
7. More resources available for ex-users
8. Tougher police action against suppliers of drugs
9. More short-term detoxification facilities
10. Tougher measures to protect drugs from being available in prison
11. Tougher police action against drug users

In addition to these some people gave us further suggestions of ways they felt addicts and users might be helped to come off drugs:

- more education about the risks and effects of taking drugs
- more care and counselling for drug users and their families and friends
- stricter control over international drug trafficking
- more self-help groups
- legalisation of cannabis
- concentration on 'hard' drugs (concern over 'soft' drugs being counter productive)

A warning comes loud and clear from the users in our survey – it is their overriding message, the reason why they completed our lengthy survey and told us so many personal details about their lives. It's a simple piece of advice from those who have experience of drug-taking to those who may be thinking about experimenting with drugs – DON'T!

Don't do it. It turns you into a liar, a thief. It ruins your life, breaks the hearts of your family, makes you ill. You become dirty and scruffy and lazy. You lose all sense of feeling and self-respect. And you die a little bit every day.

My advice would be to stay clear of places where drugs are used or on sale. If you are thinking of starting – don't. You have got to be strong when being pressurised into it.

101

Remember when people pass you a joint or a pill or whatever, they are in fact saying, 'let me spoil your life.'

If you've not started then don't try. Resist the temptation by moving on to a different scene where drugs aren't the norm. Their danger is they are so much fun when you're with a crowd of friends and that's how you can so easily start taking them.

Don't start because there's no stopping.

That's all good advice, particularly good because it comes from people who have taken or are still taking drugs. They are the experts after all – they know what drugs have done to their lives.

However, a number of those people had different views on cannabis.

Stay off *hard* drugs! There's nothing wrong with smoking hash in moderation. I know it's a damn sight better than alcohol. Don't listen to people who say you would feel a lot better if you took drugs. Don't do anything for anyone but yourself. Always remember you are the one who reaps the harvest of your deeds. Never rely on an addict for help when you need it.

I think it is completely misleading and irrelevant to put cannabis in the same class as most other drugs. There is absolutely no comparison between cannabis and the effects, dangers and addictiveness of most other drugs. At the same time I think people should realise that it isn't just heroin which is addictive and that the rest are 'safe'. It's not true, the others aren't safe and they can be just as addictive.

But as we have seen from the survey cannabis can lead to problems and in some cases can create certain kinds of addicts:

I think cannabis is probably okay but it is easy to become mentally addicted despite the popular belief that cannabis is non-addictive.

Never get into a situation where you take it regularly because anyone can develop a habit for it and you can become addicted.

Drugs are a frightening subject. The effects of taking them regularly for most people are very disturbing. The advice of ex-addicts in our survey to current users was clear:

Kick it all in before it gets too heavy. It nearly always leads to crime, hospital, prison and sometimes death. Since last year most of the drug addicts I know are locked up or in hospital. One of them is dead.

And if you want help now, what can you do? One man who was a heroin addict told us:

If you want to stop then you must pester everyone to get help. That way someone might just listen. It's your life. You don't have to waste it. Pester and pester people until you get help and get off.

And those who want to come off need encouragement:

There needs to be more emphasis on the fact that people who are addicted to drugs can and do get off. Junkies need help. They need to know that they're not bound to be failures. They need encouragement from the police, the courts and the authorities; not just punishment, but help and rehabilitation.

And in general, people's approach towards drug users and addicts came in for criticism:

I feel that the sooner the people in this country realise that probably half or more of the petty crimes and muggings occur because users need money to pay for their drugs it would help people understand the real problem of drug abuse and addiction. These people need specialist help and treatment centres. They've got involved in crime because of their drugs not because they started as criminals. If you want to stop them from being criminals then you either have to treat those who are already hooked and make them not want to touch the stuff again, or, for those who might be tempted into starting, you have to remove their desire to experiment and play with these drugs in the first place.

The fact that possession of most of the drugs we've talked about is in itself a crime also came in for criticism.

I think the laws on drugs should be changed so that users aren't breaking the law for possessing drugs. Supplying them is different – that should stay illegal. But the present legal system just makes the drugs scene far more difficult to deal with and makes many regular users and addicts afraid to come and get help.

But should drugs, or some drugs, like cannabis, be legalised? In our national poll we asked people what they thought. Nearly seven out of every ten people we asked said 'no'. The remainder didn't know or didn't want to say and just one in ten people thought it should be legalised.

But the fact that the drugs he was addicted to – tranquillisers – were legal was little comfort to this man. He told us:

I'm fifty-two years old and I feel I've aged more than I should have. Drugs have ruined my life, my health and my marriage.

Drugs have taken away my ability to cope. I was never told that taking drugs would have long term effects – doctors simply prescribed them as and when I wanted them and without any idea of the consequences to my life.

For many people drugs are a crutch. They take drugs

104

regularly, because drugs fill a hole in their lives. As one man who was addicted to cannabis told us:

> As a social habit think twice. But if you have a problem and you think that drugs might help, don't take them. Deal with the problem. Don't try to escape from it by using drugs or alcohol. It won't take away the problem. It will just give you another.

And another man told us:

> I believe I was very lucky in my escape. Drugs are really unnecessary. I believe you should ask yourself why you want to take a drug. If it's for a problem then the cause needs treating. If it's just because it's available and your friends take it – as happened with me – then you need to think twice before you say yes. Ask yourself why you're saying yes before you smoke and then you'll be able to just say no.

Just Saying No is one answer to the drug problem. For those who haven't yet started we need effective preventive education in schools, at home and in the community as a whole. But for those already on drugs we have to make sure that society has something to offer them in place of drugs:

> When you're involved with drugs and the drug scene, every friend you have is a user. To get off you have to be able to break away from that drug scene and those friends. You have to lose your friends' company if they take drugs – despite the fact that this will be a time when you need friends most. If you continue to see them then temptation will stare you straight in the face and you'll probably start taking them again.

But it's not only friends. It's a way of life and you need to change your lifestyle if you are going to come off. But for how many people is this a realistic option?

One user told us:

> Everyone needs to feel wanted. But when society rejects a whole generation as it is doing at the moment it's hard not to see why the drug problem persists and continues to grow. Young people need to feel wanted. They need a sense of optimism for the future. It's part of human nature to strive for something better in the future. When there is no hope what is the point of living?

There aren't any miracle solutions to the drug problem. But we hope that the information which all our drug users have provided will help people come closer to understanding the problem and knock down some of the myths about drug-taking.

When we first announced the survey on *That's Life* one boy wrote:

> My parents only found out that I was taking drugs when you said on television that you were doing this survey. Then my Mum turned to me and said, 'Thank God that you've never taken drugs.' I said, 'I have.'

He told us he wished he hadn't started but was glad at least that his drug use was out in the open and that he could talk about it with his family. If *Drugwatch* achieves no more than helping families talk about drugs and providing them with a more informed framework in which to discuss the problem, then it will have more than fulfilled its purpose.

SECTION III

HOW TO GET TREATMENT AND HELP

By Dr John Strang and David Turner

In some parts of the country there are special services for people with drug problems. But in many places there are no special services. This section is meant to assist you to get the best help possible whether or not you have a special service nearby. It won't necessarily give you all the answers, but we hope that it will make it easier to use what services there are.

The first part of this section quotes questions which are often asked by people who have tried to get help and failed. The answers may help you in future to get an appropriate service. The second part tells you about the types of special service which are available, what they do and how to get help from them. By knowing more about what does or does not exist, you can think about what it is you want *before* you look for help. Often the service you get will have to be put together specially for you, so working out first what you want realistically is important. And remember that all the services are to help people get off drugs, not keep on using them.

There is no treatment available where I live

The health service is organised into Regions – the Regional Health Authorities – and in each region there are Districts – the District Health Authorities. Regions cover several counties, Districts a town, part of a city or part of a county. The government has told the Regions and Districts that they should provide treatment for people with drug problems. They did this by sending official letters to all the Regions and Districts first in 1982 (know as HC82/12) and again in 1984 (known as HC84/14). The second letter said help for people with drug problems was a priority, all the Districts should make sure they knew what the size of the drug problem in their District was, that they should make sure help was available and tell the government what their plans were. If you find out that there is no treatment available, you should ask your District why not and what their plans are to make it available.

You may know if there is a local treatment service. You can find out either by asking your family doctor, the Citizens Advice Bureau or by contacting SCODA. The address is at the back of this section.

But it's not something that my family doctor or a general doctor can do anything about – it's a job for a drug specialist

All doctors have a responsibility to care for the health of their patients – including their drug problems. As more people use drugs like heroin, it is likely that most will be ordinary people living at home or where they have lived for a long time. So many will go to their family doctors first to try to get help. It is more sensible for non-specialist doctors to help those with drug problems, sending the more difficult patients to drug specialists.

At the end of 1984, the government published 'Guidelines of Good Clinical Practice in the Treatment of Drug Misuse'. This described how family doctors and general hospital doctors could help people with drug problems. It explained that a straightforward drug withdrawal was the sort of thing that any doctor could arrange – not just specialists, and told them how they could help patients who misused illegal drugs. Every doctor in the country should have been sent a copy of the 'Guidelines'. As well as these Guidelines, an excellent book called *Drug Addiction and Polydrug Abuse – The Role of the General Practitioner* has been written by two family doctors, Dr Banks and Dr Waller. It is published by the Institue for the Study of Drug Dependence (ISDD). Their address is at the back of this guide.

But surely only a specially licensed doctor can prescribe a drug withdrawal

Only specially licensed doctors can prescribe heroin, cocaine and dipipanone (which is part of a drug known as Diconal) to drug addicts. But it's very unlikely that a doctor would agree to prescribe any of these drugs to an addict and it's very rare for even a specially licensed doctor to prescribe them.

The Guidelines for doctors recommend the use of a slow acting drug called Methadone for drug withdrawal from heroin and similar drugs. It comes in a syrup form and is designed to be taken orally. It can be prescribed by any qualified doctor, but particular care has to be taken in prescribing and dispensing it. The law allows a family doctor or general doctor to prescribe a drug withdrawal using Methadone. The normal way is for a daily supply to be given with the daily amount tailing down to zero over a month or two. The details of this are given in the 'Guidelines' and in the book by Dr Banks and Dr Waller.

Of course doctors will not want to make the mistake of becoming involved in careless prescribing. They will want to be cautious and may well need safeguards to be included to make sure that the drugs they prescribe are not misused. But they can prescribe a drug withdrawal and have been advised about how to do it.

But I don't want to be notified to the police

When you go to the doctor, you are protected by the same rules of confidentiality that protect all patients. Your doctor is not allowed to tell anyone else – your employer, the police or your family – about your drug use. It may be suggested that you should tell them yourself so they can help you in your drug withdrawal.

People have become confused because there is a system of notification. A doctor has to complete a form on each patient seen who is addicted to opiates. This is kept to help assess the size of the drug problem. No personal information from this notification is available to anyone but a doctor, and even then careful checks are made to ensure that the doctor really needs the information. In other words, the police, drug squads, your employer, family, visa departments, and so on cannot get this information.

All doctors, whether they are working in the NHS or are private doctors, have to complete a notification form on patients they see who are addicted to opiates.

What's all this about getting registered?

There is a belief that those with drug problems can enroll at a special drug clinic and then automatically get any drugs they choose from the clinic. *This is false* – no such system exists.

I've been told to pull myself together and do it on my own

It's possible to bring yourself off drugs on your own, but it is more difficult. You have to control what you are taking first, and then steadily reduce it down to zero so that you don't experience severe withdrawal symptoms. In effect, you are just tackling the task bit by bit. If a doctor is prescribing a drug withdrawal to you, then essentially he is helping you to avoid withdrawal symptoms. Giving up drugs all at once may result in you going back to drugs because you don't like the withdrawal symptoms.

If you've been told 'just pull yourself together', you may wish to follow up on some of the suggestions in this section to help prepare your own plan and then go back to your doctor to discuss it. If this fails, you can ask your doctor to refer you for a second opinion. If all else fails, it may be worth thinking of changing your doctor.

Without a doctor's help, surely it's impossible to get off drugs?

Not at all. Like many changes which people need to make, success depends largely on the person's determination and planning, but of course other people and services can help.

Some people have gone through abrupt withdrawal (cold turkey) and have managed to become drug-free. But it's probably best to try and arrange a drug withdrawal, even if you have to do it yourself by steadily reducing your daily dose to zero over a planned period of time. Obviously it is easier if someone is helping you, but you can do it alone.

The Blenheim Project in London has published two short guides – 'How to Stop', for people wanting to get off opiates, and 'How to Help', for parents, relatives and friends. Each costs 50p and can be bought from ISDD. You may find it helpful to use them in planning your drug withdrawal.

But I've been told that I have no right to a service because it is a self-inflicted condition

This is no ground for refusal of help. If you have been told this, you should quote the official letters mentioned at the start of this section

Many conditions treated by doctors have at least some self-inflicted quality to them – accidents after drinking alcohol, bronchitis and cancer from smoking, injuries whilst mountain climbing or sailing – but that is not a reason for refusing treatment.

But my doctor thinks I'm just after drugs

Doctors are understandably nervous about people with drug problems because some people have sought help merely in order to obtain a free supply of drugs. Probably the best way to deal with this is to put together a realistic plan with safeguards so that your doctor can be sure you are keeping to the plan. For example, agree on the rate at which you will reduce your daily drug use during drug withdrawal; agree on how long the withdrawal will take to be completed; agree how often you will attend the surgery during drug withdrawal; agree on regular physical examinations and urine testing for drugs. It's often a good idea to plan other changes in your life around the same time, doing something which you have wanted to do but your drug use made impossible. For instance, you could get involved in new work or training, move out of the area for a while and stay with relatives, take up a sport or hobby, join some club or activity away from drug-using friends. All this will help to show your doctor that you really want to make changes and stop using drugs.

111

My doctor point blank refuses to do anything for me

If you have tried everything already suggested, it might be best to change your doctor. But it may be that your doctor thinks your plans are unrealistic. If this is the case, he should discuss this with you and look at what other plans might be more realistic – for example, in-patient treatment or a rehabilitation house.

Can I choose what treatment I want?

Yes and no. It's obviously important that you are involved in discussing realistic plans to tackle your drug problem. But it is the responsibility of the doctor to decide what medical treatments he thinks are appropriate in your particular case – and the doctor is required to justify his prescribing of controlled drugs. It is not just a matter of choosing a treatment from a shopping list of possibilities. What should happen is that you and your doctor discuss which options seem best and agree a plan which seems most relevant for you.

Can I turn up at hospital as an emergency patient?

In general, casualty departments don't regard help for dependence on drugs as an emergency. Of course this is different if it involves drug overdose or if severe drug withdrawal symptoms have developed. Emergency treatment may then be essential.

If you are looking for treatment for drug dependence, it is best to get it through your family doctor or special treatment service, not to try to get it through the casualty department.

GETTING HELP

First, work out what service you want. Broadly, services fall into one of three groups – medical, social or legal. You may want help from more than one service, but it's probably helpful to consider them one at a time.

Medical Services

If you want medical help, your first port of call will almost inevitably be your family doctor or a member of staff at the local health centre. If you have a general health problem you should tell your doctor about your drug taking. The information might be important in deciding the right treatment, for instance, if you have hepatitis or are pregnant. If you are seeking help with your drug problem, the treatment you get will largely depend on the help you ask for and how you ask for it. Most doctors feel that there is little they can do unless you want to stop taking drugs apart from giving you general advice and general medical care. If there is a hospital drug treatment centre available locally, your doctor may refer you to it to get specialist help.

The hospital treatment centres vary in what they can offer. Most have full time staff including a psychiatrist, nurse and social worker. A referral letter from your doctor is needed usually and it may take a few weeks before you get an appointment date. You will be expected to go to the treatment centre regularly and to have a urine test when you go there. Methadone may be prescribed over a longer period of time than your family doctor will prescribe for, but you will still be expected to gradually stop using drugs, probably over a six-month period. Because the treatment centres are there specially for those with drug problems, the staff have more experience and can give more time to you. They are particularly helpful for people who have difficulty in giving up drugs quite quickly and need a lot of help to work out how they are going to live without them.

It is likely, even if there is a local hospital treatment centre that you will still need the help of your family doctor. So you might try to come off drugs using that help. If this is the case decide whether it is realistic to stop using while still living at home. What support will you need? Should you make regular appointments for counselling/psychotherapy – either alone or with your family? During drug withdrawal, who will look after the drugs so that they are taken according to the plan you have agreed with your doctor? How long will the drug withdrawal take? Do you need a drug withdrawal or could you manage to stop on your own if you have a small supply of tablets to help you sleep? If you are using a drug withdrawal with Methadone or with tablets for sleeping, make sure that it is for a short time with a clear end in sight. There's no point just swapping from one drug to another.

Whether your plan is realistic or not will depend on how much drugs you have been taking, how often and for how long; on the support you can get from your family, friends and work; where you live; what you are going to do instead of taking drugs. And at the end of the day, it will depend on what service is provided locally.

If your plan seems unrealistic despite all these arrangements, then you need to look at ways of making it more watertight. Could you stay with friends or relatives while going through withdrawal? Should you move away from where you live? How will you make new, non-drug-taking friends and break away from your drug-taking friends? What can you get involved in to fill the 'hole' that will be left when you give up drugs – training or work, new interests/hobbies and so on.

Perhaps the plan still seems unrealistic. Then you and your doctor might consider in-patient withdrawal from drugs. This may be at a special hospital unit, but because of the shortage of these, it may be in the local general hospital where you stay for a few weeks while you undergo withdrawal. This will probably be on a general psychiatric short stay ward. The 'Guidelines' explain gradual withdrawal arrangements for general hospital doctors. As an in-patient it is almost always possible to come off drugs in a matter of weeks. However, you should include in your plans means of getting other support and help. The changes to your life mentioned above will still be needed if you are going to stay off drugs. Getting off is just the first step, staying off is as important and needs to be included in your plans.

If you have been particularly heavily involved in drugs, or have had problems in breaking your habit and dependence on drugs, you should consider going in to one of the few NHS special patient units or a drug-free rehabilitation house. In these you will normally be a resident for up to a year and they are there specifically to help people to learn to live without drugs. The rehabilitation houses are described below.

Social and Legal Services

If you are undecided about what help you want, or you don't think you need medical help but have problems which you want to deal with, you may go to one of the day time services. In some parts of the country there are specialist day time services for people with drug problems. These may be run by a voluntary organisation, by the local authority or by the health authority. You will usually have to ring to make an appointment, but this can be done very quickly. The appointment is made to make sure that you are seen straight away rather than having to wait for a long time.

The specialist day time services provide couselling and support. This can be very important if you can't decide what you want to do about your drug problem and need someone to talk over the options with. If you want to stop taking drugs, the support they can give you will be an important part of your drug withdrawal plan. Before you can think of making what seems like a major change in your life, you may want to sort out some of the other problems you have. The day time services will be able to help you deal with these, either themselves or by putting you in touch with the right service.

If you are in an area where there is no specialist day time service, you can still get help. Work out what the problem is and what sort of help you want. If it is support whilst you go through drug withdrawal, then a private counsellor or psychotherapist might be helpful. You can get the name and address of a local one from the British Association for Counselling. Their address is at the end of this section. If you have a housing problem, you can go to the local Housing Advice Centre, the local authority Housing Department or the Citizens Advice Bureau. If you have problems with social security, there might be a local Social Security/Benefits Advisory Service, or the Citizens Advice Bureau will be able to help. The important thing to remember is that just because you have a drug problem you are not excluded from getting the same help from these services as everybody else is entitled to.

In some parts of the country, mainly the south of England, self help groups have been formed to help people with drug problems keep drug-free. As well as using the other services mentioned, you might find such a group helpful to you and either want to join one, or to form one. If so, then contact Narcotics Anonymous. Their address and telephone number is at the back of this section.

Many drug takers get in to trouble with the law. You are entitled to legal advice from a qualified solicitor and may be entitled to free legal aid if you are charged with an offence. If you do get arrested, and it happens several times, you may well think about giving up drugs. The problems you have will not go away, and continuing to take drugs will probably mean getting arrested again. Release, a drug agency based in London, provides a national 24 hour emergency telephone service particularly for people who have been arrested. Their emergency telephone number is given at the back of this section.

Because some people cannot stop taking drugs or remain drug-free whilst living at home surrounded by people still taking drugs, drug-free rehabilitation houses exist up and

116

down the country where people can learn new ways to live without drugs. In general, these houses can be divided into four categories:

1. Concept Houses – where there is a clear hierarchical structure so that you will work progressively through a programme, being given more responsibility for yourself and others as you progress. You are expected to work in and for the community. Part of the programme involves intensive group therapy sessions as well as group activities.

2. General Houses – where there is a more community oriented approach. The emphasis is on learning to live together in a supportive community, individual and group counselling and preparing for work or further training.

3. Houses with Christian Staff – are similar to the General Houses. The staff maintain a Christian belief but do not demand similar belief from residents.

4. Christian Philosophy Houses – where the programme may be similar to either the Concept Houses or the General Houses, but where an essential ingredient in the programme is the acceptance by the resident of Jesus as Lord.

Most of the rehabilitation houses expect a resident to stay for a year or longer. Nearly all provide a support structure to help the resident on leaving the main rehabilitation house.

The cost of staying at the rehabilitation houses is largely met by Supplementary Benefits, but this doesn't cover the whole cost. The local authority Social Services Department is usually expected to pay something towards the cost. This is often difficult to get, the only answer is persistence and enlisting the help of your doctor, probation officer, and Councillor.

If you are living with your family, with a partner, or have a family of your own, they may also want advice, help and support. This will be all the more important if you want them to assist you to stop taking drugs. All the specialist day time services can provide this help. Some of these services and some of the hospital treatment centres run support groups for relatives and partners. There are also self-help groups run independently of other services, such as 'Drug-lines' and 'Families Anonymous'. From the *Drugwatch* programme, we hope many more such groups will be formed. If you would like to contact one in your area, the address of the nearest group is available from SCODA.

Information about all the specialist services for people with drug problems can be obtained from SCODA. Their address is at the end of this section.

If you get stuck at one particular stage, don't give up. You may need to re-think your plan and perhaps change the service you are using or your doctor.

If you think that the service you have been getting has been poor, then there is no reason why you shouldn't make a formal complaint. Before you do this, however, make sure that you have been sticking to what you promised in your plan and if you haven't, that you discussed possible changes to your plan and the reasons for them with the service before you put them into action.

If you are unhappy with the teatment you are getting from your doctor, you can ask to be referred for a second opinion to the local drug clinic if there is one, or to the local psychiatric service. Or you may want to change your doctor, in which case you can ask the Family Practitioner Committee to allocate you to a new doctor. But there is no guarantee that your new doctor will give you what you want.

If the local hospital does not seem to be taking your case seriously, you may want to contact the hospital adminis-trator or the District Medical Officer at the District Health Authority. If you feel there is still no progress, then it may be worth contacting the General Manager of the health author-ity. It is a good idea to write to these people as well as telephoning, date the letter and keep a copy. Don't lose your temper but try to keep up persistent reasonable pressure for an appropriate service to be provided for people with drug problems.

Other alternatives you might use are the local Community Health Council – which is the patient's watchdog over local services, your local Borough or County Councillor, your Member of Parliament and in extreme cases, the Health Service Ombudsman.

Points to Remember
The health service is there to care for the health needs of everyone, including people with drug problems. The government has told health authorities to make services for drug users a priority.

But in many Districts, there is as yet no recognised service for people with drug problems. In getting help for yourself, the services which are there will need to adapt themselves to the needs of drug users. As a result, the help you eventually receive may be provided under some other 'label' and not identified as a drug service.

Most services, whether specialist or not, are much more sympathetic to your needs if they feel that you have given some thought to what you want to achieve and how you might do so. If you have no real plans, or they are very loose and unclear, it doesn't help them when trying to give you a good service and it doesn't help you. It's not surprising in such circumstances if they are not happy to accept you as a client or patient.

When you think about your plan for giving up drugs, write it down. See if there are gaps in it. And ask the advice of the people you want to help you make it work. The plan should include:

1. How you will switch from your present use of drugs – which may be from the black market – to a more controlled use, probably taking Methadone.

2. How quickly you are going to reduce your daily drug intake so that you become drug-free.

3.   What safeguards you are going to use to make sure you stick to the drug withdrawal plan you have worked out.

4.   How you are going to get the support you need both during your drug withdrawal and after it is completed so that you stay drug-free.

5.   How you are going to make the changes to your life which will break your contacts with drug-taking friends and fill the 'hole' left by giving up drugs.

SOME USEFUL ADDRESSES

SCODA (The Standing Conference on Drug Abuse)

1–4 Hatton Place, Hatton Garden, London EC1N 8ND

It is the national co-ordinating organisation for services for people with drug problems. It supplies lists of all the specialist services available throughout the country. Send a large stamped addressed envelope with your request for information about your local services.

ISDD (The Institute for the Study of Drug Dependence)

1–4 Hatton Place, Hatton Garden, London EC1N 8ND

It is a library and information service about drug misuse. They publish material about drugs and sell publications for other organisations. Write to them for a list of the publications they have and the prices.

British Association for Counselling

87a Sheep Street, Rugby, Warwicks CV21 3BX

It can put you in touch with a local counsellor/psychotherapist. Include a stamped addressed envelope for their reply.

NAYPCAS (The National Associaton of Young People's Counselling and Advisory Services)

17–23 Albion Street, Leicester LE1 6 GD

It can put you in touch with a local youth counselling

service. These are usually for people under 21. Include a stamped addressed envelope.

Narcotics Anonymous

PO Box 246, c/o 47 Milman Street, London SW10 Tel: 01 351 6794

They can tell you where the nearest meeting is held or help you to start your own self-help group for people with drug problems. The telephone uses an answering machine to take messages and there is usually someone there between 2.30 p.m. and 8 p.m. each weekday.

Release

Advice on legal problems arising from drug misuse. Outside normal working hours and at weekends, there is an emergency telephone service. When you dial the number, the operator intercepts the call and gives you another number to ring. There is always someone there to answer your call in person. The emergency telephone number is: 01 603 8654

Special note for people living in Scotland

Throughout this section the terms District Health Authority and Regional Health Authority are used. In Scotland, the health service is slightly differently organised. Health Districts and Health Boards are the same as Health Districts and Health Regions in England. If you change the names, the information about how to get help is accurate for both Scotland and England.

The official letters which went to Health Boards in Scotland were sent by the Scottish Home and Health Department. The Scottish Health Authorities' Priorities for the Eighties (SHAPE) Report gave priority to services for people with drug problems. And a second letter asked Health Boards to give the Scottish Office detailed information about their plans. If you find that there is no treatment available, you should ask your district or Health Board why not, and what their plans are to make it available. You can quote these official letters to them.

Special note for people living in Wales

Throughout this section, the terms district Health Authority and Regional Health Authority are used. In Wales there is no Regional Health Authority, and the Welsh Office in Cardiff is the Regional Authority. There are District Health Authorities. If you change the names, the information about how to get help is accurate for both Wales and England.

The Welsh Office has sent an official letter to the District Health Authorities similar to the one sent in England by the government. If you find that there is no treatment available, you should ask your District why not, and what their plans are to make it available.

THE SURVEY

THAT'S LIFE DRUGS SURVEY – USERS' QUESTIONNAIRE

Full Name ....

Address..

....

Postcode...

Tel No ....

Daytime Tel No (if different) ....

Sex   Male 54%,   Female 46%

Age

About this questionnaire

This questionnaire is in four sections.

The first section asks whether you are taking drugs now and about the *first* drugs you ever took.

The second section asks about the drugs you are or were most heavily involved with and that you took most regularly. We also ask about your life when you were taking drugs most regularly. This may, of course, be now.

The third section asks about any help, advice or treatment you may have tried to get and what you received – and we also ask about trying to stop taking drugs on your own.

The final section asks about your personal circumstances and views about drug taking.

How to answer this questionnaire

For many questions you need only put a tick in the box provided, alongside the answer that is right for you. For other questions, please write in your answer in the space provided. If there are questions which do not apply to you or which you do not wish to answer – or indeed you can't remember, please leave them unmarked.

The drugs we shall be asking you about
We are interested in finding out about the drugs on this list which have not been prescribed by a doctor. We are also interested in drugs that you may have got by prescription to treat a drug problem.

If you have taken a drug which does not appear on this list or which is a combination of a number of other drugs, please tell us what that drug is in the space provided at the bottom of this page.

Please tick which drugs you have ever taken

Average number taken:
10 different drugs

Opiates	Heroin ('H', 'Smack', 'Skag') **48%**
	Methadone (Physeptone amps, tablets, linctus, mixture) **40%**
	Diconal ('Dikes') **32%**
	DF118 **36%**
	Morphine **34%**
	Pethidine **26%**
	Opium **44%**
	Palfium **19%**
Sedatives	Barbiturates (Tuinal, Nembutal, Seconal, etc.) **47%**
	Benzodiazepines (Valium, Librium, Mogadon, Ativan, etc.) **67%**
	Other 'sleepers or downers' (Mandrax, Doriden, Heminevrin, Chloral) **48%**

Stimulants	Cocaine ('Coke', 'Charlie') **60%**
	Amphetamines ('Sulphate', 'Speed') **80%**
	Pills (Dexedrine, 'Blues', 'Speed') **66%**
	Ritalin ('Rit') **18%**
	Other stimulants (Tenuate Dospan, Pemoline, etc.) **27%**
Solvents	Glues, Butane products (gas lighter fuels, etc.) **22%**
Hallucinogens	LSD **72%**
	Mushrooms **63%**
Cannabis	('Hash', 'Grass') **92%**

Other drugs you have ever taken............................

....

Section 1: Drugs now – and the first drug you ever took

1. Are you taking drugs now?
      Yes **54%**, No **46%**

If yes, what drugs have you taken in the past 4 weeks and how often have you taken them in the past 4 weeks?

Cannabis	**76%**
Stimulants	**40%**
Opiates	**39%**
Sedatives	**21%**
Hallucinogens	**11%**
Solvents	**2%**

How much of each drug do you take in a typical week and how do you take it (eg: inject, smoke, swallow, snort or other)?

Name of drug	How taken	Amount per day/week

59% are taking more than one drug ....
....
....

And how much do you spend on drugs in a typical week?

£ ....

2. What was the *first* drug you ever took?
    Name of drug ....
       Cannabis **59%**
       Stimulants **12%**
       Opiates **2%**
       Sedatives **11%**
       Hallucinogens **5%**
       Solvents **4%**
    Age when you *first* took it – average age 16
    (Under 12, **4%**; 12–14, **27%**; 15–18, **50%**)

3. Where were you living at the time?
    Name of city/town/village ....

4. Where you living in
       A privately rented house or flat **19%**
       A council housing estate **21%**
       Other council housing **7%**
       Your own house or flat **14%**
       Other (please specify) **33%**
       Parent's home **33%**
       In care **1%**
       Squat **1%**
       Nurses home, army **3%**
       Holiday **1%**

5. Were you living
   Alone **7%**
   With a partner/husband/wife **8%**
   With friends **10%**
   With your family **72%**
   Other (please specify) **3%**

   ....
   ....

6. Who did you get your first drugs from?
   A friend
   (including boyfriend, girlfriend, spouse) **72%**
   Your family **5%**
   A dealer (not a friend) **10%**
   A doctor **9%**
   Other (please specify)

   ....
   ....

7. Where did you get your first drugs?
   At school **11%**
   At a youth club **2%**
   At someone's house
   (including your own) **38%**
   At a pub **12%**
   At a disco/nightclub **7%**
   At a party **11%**
   On the street **13%**
   Other (please specify) **7%**

   ....
   ....

8. At the time, were you
   At school **50%**
   At college or university **7%**
   Employed **28%**
   Unemployed **11%**

Housewife 5%
Other (please specify)
....
....

9. At the time, what job, if any, did your mother do? If
    your mother was retired or unemployed, please give
    details of the most recent job she did.
    ....
    ....

10. At the time, what job, if any, did your father do? If your
    father was retired or unemployed, please give details of
    the most recent job he did.
    ....
    ....

11. What did you think about drug taking *before* you
    actually started taking drugs?
    No views 35%
    Positive views about drugs 29%
    Negative views about drugs 36%
    ....
    ....

12. What prompted you to start taking drugs?
    Friends 54%
    Curiosity 36%
    Problems 20%
    Glamour 13%
    Traumatic event 5%
    [some users gave more than one reason]
    ....
    ....

Section 2: Taking drugs regularly
In this section we are interested in the drug you are or were
most involved with *and* that you took most regularly. This
may, of course, be now.

13. When taking drugs most regularly what drugs are (were) you using and how much of each drug are (were) you taking?

Name of drug   Amount per week/month

....
....
....

14. Which *one* drug are (were) you most involved with?
Name of drug
    Cannabis **32%**
    Heroin **26%**
    Speed **13%**
    LSD **5%**
    Tranquillisers **5%**
    Cocaine **3%**
    Solvents **3%**

Please answer the remaining questions in this section in respect of *this* drug.

15. How do (did) you take this drug?
    Inject the drug **31%**
    Smoke the drug **51%**
    Swallow the drug **36%**
    Snort or sniff the drug **22%**
    Others (please specify)
[the same drug may be taken in different ways.]

....
....

16. Who did you first get this drug from?
    A friend **70%**
    Your family **3%**
    A dealer (not a friend) **17%**
    A doctor **10%**
    Other (please specify)

....
....

17. Who were you with when you first used this drug?
    Your best friend 26%
    A group of people, including
    good friends 54%
    A group of people, but no
    good friends 9%
    Strangers 3%
    Alone 9%
    Other (please specify)

    ....
    ....

18. If you were with anyone else, were they regular users of
    that drug?
    Yes, all of them 32%
    Yes, but not all of them 42%
    No, none of them 11%
    (15% didn't state)

19. Describe that first occasion (eg: was it a party, did you
    intend to try the drug, were you pressured into trying
    the drug, was it a good experience or a bad one, was it
    what you expected? etc.)
    70% enjoyed the experience
    13% felt ill or sick
    9% had not enjoyed the experience

20. At the time did you think you would use this drug
    again?
    Yes 70%   No 28%   2% not stated
    If no, why did you use the drug again? Please explain.
    'friends' – overwhelmingly the reason given

    ....
    ....

21. How soon after the first use did you start to use the
    drug regularly?
    Within _____ weeks (approximately)
    31% within 1 week

31% within 1 month
16% within 1–3 months
4% within 3–6 months
13% over 6 months
5% not stated

22. When using drugs most regularly, who do (did) you get this drug from?
A friend **54%**
Your family **1%**
A dealer (not a friend) **46%**
A doctor **16%**
Other (please specify) **2%**
[Obviously user gets drug from more than one source]
....
....

23. And where do (did) you get this drug?
At school **4%**
At a youth club **3%**
At someone's house
(including your own) **61%**
At a pub **29%**
At a disco/nightclub **10%**
At parties **14%**
On the street **23%**
Other (please specify).
....
....

24. How much money in total are (were) you spending on drugs in a typical week when using most regularly.
£82.45 (average amount spent per week.)

Was this more than you could afford?
Yes **55%** No **45%**

Please explain.
....
....

25. What is (was) your main source of income?
   Parents **12%**
   Friends **6%**
   Wages/salary
   (your own or your partner's) **52%**
   Savings/private income **6%**
   Social Security/other benefits **38%**
   Theft **23%**
   Drug dealing **21%**
   Prostitution **4%**
   Borrowing **16%**
   Other (please specify)

   . . . .
   . . . .

26. When using drugs most regularly, are (were) you living
   Alone **20%**
   With a partner/husband/wife **36%**
   With friends **26%**
   With parents **27%**
   Other (please specify)
 [Total is greater than 100% because users may have lived with more than one of these]

27. And, where are (were) you living?
 Name of city/town/village _____

28. Are (were) most of your friends also using the drug regularly?
   Yes **73%** No **27%**

29. At the time, are (were) you
   At school **13%**
   At college or university **8%**
   Employed **43%**
   Unemployed **40%**
   Housewife **7%**
   Other (please specify)

   . . . .
   . . . .

30. Do you feel you are (were) addicted to the drug you are (were) most heavily involved with?

    Yes   No

        Cannabis **13**%
        Speed **70**%
        Cocaine **83**%
        Heroin **95**%

If yes, how long after you *first* took that drug did you feel you became addicted?

    Within three months
        Cannabis **0**%
        Speed **38**%
        Cocaine **45**%
        Heroin **55**%

And, what made you think you were addicted. Please describe:

    'withdrawal symptoms'
    'incapable without drugs'
    'experienced panic'
    'nervous/paranoid'
    'mental addiction'
    'craving/need for drugs'
    'obsessed by drugs'
    'someone else told me'

    ....
    ....

31. How has taking drugs affected your life (your family, your job, your health, etc.)?

    'health problems'
    'upset family'
    'work problems'
    'no ill effects'
    'mental problems'
    'good effects'
    'ruined life'
    'strain on marriage'
    'lost friends'

    ....
    ....

32. Please describe your local drug scene (what drugs are being used in your area and what drugs are available; what's the local slang for these drugs and how much do they cost; how old are the people who are mainly using drugs? etc.).

....
....
....

Section 3: Getting Help

33. Have you ever worried about taking drugs?
    Yes **71%**   No **28%**
    If yes, what worried (worries) you most? (Please tick only *one*.)
    Scared of becoming a junkie **26%**
    Didn't know how you were
    going to pay for the drugs **25%**
    It would ruin your health **35%**
    It would ruin your job prospects **12%**
    That it was illegal **17%**
    Other (please specify)

    ....
    ....

34. At any time did you ask your family or friends for help?
    Yes **33%**   No **64%**

        Cannabis **4%**
        Speed **37%**
        Heroin **56%**
    If yes, what help did they give you?
    'moral support'
    'practical help'
    'financial help'
    'gave a home'
    'advice'

    ....
    ....

135

35. Did you seek professional help?
          Yes 50%   No 50%

          Heroin 82%
          Speed 50%
          Cannabis 17%
     If yes, was it because
          Of family pressure 25%
          You felt ill 43%
          You felt frightened 41%
          Your job was threatened 8%
          You had been arrested 25%
          The death of a friend through drugs 16%
          Other (please specify)

     ....
     ....

36. Who did you contact *first*? (Please tick only *one*.)
          Your GP 65%
          A teacher 1%
          A social worker 8%
          A vicar or minister of religion 5%
          A drugs organisation 18%
          psychiatrist 3%
          Other (please specify)

     ....
     ....

37. Generally, what help or advice have you been given?
          'no help'
          'not much help'
          'being prescribed drugs'
          'being told to stop'
          'go to your GP'

38. Were you satisfied with that help or advice?
          Yes 44%   No 56%
     Why?

     ....
     ....

39. If you went to your GP for help, was the doctor helpful?
       Yes 41%   No 49%
    Please explain why?
       ....
       ....

40. Have you ever tried to get any form of specialised treatment to get you off drugs?
       Yes 35%   No 65%
    If no, why not?
    If yes, what difficulties, if any, did you encounter?
       ....
       ....

41. Did you get treatment straightaway?
       Yes 41%   No 59%
    If no, how long did you have to wait?
       _____ months (approximately)

42. What was the *first* sort of treatment you had? Please describe it and say how effective it was for you.
       other prescribed drugs
       hospitalization
       ....
       ....

43. Have you had treatment(s) since?
       Yes 50%   No 50%
    If yes, please describe it and say how effective it (they) was (were) for you.
       ....
       ....

137

44. If you were ever prescribed methadone as part of an out-patient treatment did your chemist agree to supply it?

   Yes **83%**

   Please describe any problems or difficulties you had in getting supplies of methadone.

   ....
   ....

45. If you managed to stop taking drugs altogether for a period of more than 3 months did you do this

   On your own **67%**
   Following a recognised form
   of treatment **19%**
   In prison **16%**
   With family's help **3%**
   God **3%**
   Drugs organisation **3%**
   Other (please specify)

   Please describe how long in total you remained off drugs – and, if you started taking drugs again please explain why.

   3–6 months **16%**
   6–12 months **16%**
   12–18 months **11%**
   18–24 months **5%**
   2–3 years **6%**
   3–5 years **7%**

   ....
   ....

Section 4: Your personal circumstances and views about drug taking

46. Does your family know about your drug use?

   Yes **74%**   No **26%**

   If yes, how did they react when they found out you were using drugs (eg: were they understanding and helpful, or did they call the police, throw you out of the

house, etc.)?
    'family helpful' **45%**
    'family upset'/'shocked' **27%**
    'not concerned'/'didn't understand' **21%**
    '*tried* to help' **13%**
    'threw user out'/'angry'/'disapproved' **21%**

47. How many brothers and sisters do you have?

. . . .

48. Are you the
    Eldest child **40%**
    Second child **27%**
    Third child **16%**
    Fourth child **7%**
    Other (eg: adopted – please specify)

. . . .

49. Before taking drugs had you ever been in serious trouble or had serious problems with any of the following?
    At school **25%**
    With the police **20%**
    With Social Services **6%**
    No serious trouble or problems
If you ticked boxes 1 to 3 please give brief details.

. . . .
. . . .

50. Since taking drugs have you had any convictions for
    Possession of drugs **29%**
    Supplying drugs **8%**
    Shoplifting **14%**
    Burglary or theft **25%**
    Assault **10%**
    Prostitution **1%**
    Other (please specify)
[**50%** of total sample had convictions]

. . . .
. . . .

51. If you have convictions for shoplifting, burglary or theft, assault, prostitution or 'other', how do these relate to drug taking? Please explain.
    80% drug-related
    40% to get money for drugs
    20% not drug-related
    10% to get drugs themselves
    30% possession

    . . . .
    . . . .

52. Since taking drugs have you ever been in prison?
    Yes **26%**   No **72%**
    If yes, did you take drugs in prison?
    Yes **15%**   No **10%**

53. Have you ever got into serious debt because of the money you were spending on drugs?
    Yes **38%**   No **62%**
    If yes, please give details.

    . . . .
    . . . .

54. Which of the following, if any, applies to your immediate family?

	Husband/ Wife/ Partner	Mother	Father
Smoke cigarettes	36%	43%	40%
Drink more than 2½ pints or 5 shorts a day	5%	5%	15%
Take tranquillisers every day	3%	11%	3%
Take any of the drugs listed on page 2 (please specify)	18%	7%	4%

. . . .
. . . .

55.	Have you ever
	Stolen from people you know
	to pay for drugs **32%**
	Stolen from strangers to pay
	for drugs **32%**
	Sold drugs on a regular basis **32%**
	Assaulted anyone as a direct
	result of taking drugs **18%**
	Been 'registered' as a drug
	addict **25%**
	Introduced friends or
	relations to drugs **49%**
	None of these **21%**

56.	Have you ever suffered from any of the following since
	using drugs?
	Withdrawal symptoms **60%**
	(please specify)

	. . . .
	. . . .

	Drug-related infection
	(eg: abcess,
	scepticaemia) **17%**
	Hepatitis (drug-related) **16%**
	Overdose **34%**
	Admission to a casualty
	department for other drug-related problems **21%**
	Other (please specify) **3%**

	. . . .
	. . . .
	None of these **33%**

57.	Do you wish you had never taken drugs?
	Yes **44%** No **54%**

58.	From your experience, what advice would you give to
	other people who are starting to, or are already taking
	drugs?
	Negative mentions **84%**

141

Positive mentions 14%
'don't'
'drugs are awful'
'drugs can change your personality'
'be careful'
'stay off hard drugs/heroin' 'cannabis OK'
'Drugs can kill'

59. Here are 3 statements about measures to help *people already taking drugs*. For each one please say whether you agree or disagree.

	Agree	Dis-agree	No opinion
Most users don't need help	21%	65%	8%
There's enough already being done to help people taking drugs	4%	85%	5%
More should be done to help users	82%	10%	6%

If you think more should be done to help drug users, which of the following measures do you think would help people already taking drugs? And which *one* would be most helpful?

1 More training for GPs in how to help drug users
2 More treatment facilities within the NHS
3 More information and advisory services for drug user's families
4 More long-term rehabilitation centres. More sympathetic response from GPs
5 Better employment prospects for ex-users
6 More resources available for ex-users
7 Tougher police actions against suppliers of drugs
8 More short-term detoxification facilities
9 Tougher police action against drug users

....
....

60. Here are 3 statements about measures to *prevent* people from *starting to take drugs*. For each one please say whether you agree or disagree.

	Agree	Dis-agree	No opinion
Most people don't need preventing	33%	48%	12%
There's enough already being done to prevent people from starting to take drugs	9%	75%	9%
More should be done to help prevent people from starting to take drugs	75%	11%	9%

If you think more should be done to help prevent people from starting to take drugs, which of the following measures do you think would help? And which *one* would be the most helpful?

1 More education about drugs in schools
2 More publicity about the dangers of drug use
3 Better job prospects for young people
4 Better communication between parents and children
5 Fewer TV programmes and articles glamourising drugs
6 Tougher police action against suppliers of drugs
7 Less liberal attitude by parents to drug use
8 Less smoking and drinking by parents of drug users
....
....
....

61. What else would you like to tell us which has not been covered and which you feel is important?

    ....
    ....
    ....
    ....

62. Finally, did you send in for this questionnaire yourself or did someone give it to you?
    Sent in for it **65%**
    Given it by someone else **32%**
    Other(please specify) **3%**

    ....
    ....